MEDITERRANEAN COOKBOOK FOR LOWERING CHOLESTEROL:

Step-by-step guide on how to lower cholesterol naturally with Easy to Make, Healthy and Delicious Recipes.

Aaron Cheney Ph.D

TABLE OF CONTENTS

CHAPTER 1 -
INTRODUCTION

7-day Mediterranean diet meal plan

Chapter 2 -
MEDITERRANEAN DIET EXPLAINED

Chapter 3-
10 MEDITERRANEAN DIET RECIPES FOR LOWERING CHOLESTEROL

Chapter 4 -
MEDITERRANEAN DIET BREAKFAST MEAL PLAN FOR LOWERING CHOLESTEROL

Chapter 5 -
MEDITERRANEAN DIET SNACKS RECIPES FOR LOWERING CHOLESTEROL

Chapter 6 -
MEDITERRANEAN DIET LUNCH MEAL PLAN AND RECIPES FOR LOWERING CHOLESTEROL

Chapter 7-
MEDITERRANEAN DIET DINNER MEAL PLAN AND RECIPES FOR LOWERING CHOLESTEROL

Chapter 8 - MEDITERRANEAN DIET DESSERTS RECIPES FOR LOWERING CHOLESTEROL

Chapter 1

INTRODUCTION

I finally left the house in November of last year to get my blood tested, something I had put off for months. The process was quick, and I received the results via email the same day. The only thing that wasn't fine was the cholesterol. My doctor advised me to change some foods in my regular diet but that, for the time being, it wasn't a serious problem. How can cholesterol be reduced? She emphasized that I should be cautious when eating eggs and limit myself to two per week. I took the diet sheet home with me, and I began eating (almost) in accordance with it.

But after that, I began crafting this tale.

Recent studies have disproved the notion that some foods, such as shrimp and eggs, increase blood cholesterol levels. But while some foods are good for us, others are bad for our cholesterol levels. Let's review the fundamentals of cholesterol before moving on to our diet.

What exactly is cholesterol you might wonder and where does it come from?
Simply put, Cholesterol is a waxy, fat-like substance produced in the liver and other cells. Cholesterol can also be defined as a biomolecule that is essential to our bodies despite its unfavorable reputation. It is a crucial part of our cells and serves as the foundation for hormones like progesterone and testosterone as well as vitamins like vitamin D. Not all cholesterol comes from the liver. Some of it originates from the things we eat. About 80% of the cholesterol required by humans' bodies is produced by their livers, with the remaining 20% coming from food. The production line within the liver is no laughing matter; it is one of the most intricate

metabolic pathways taking place within our bodies, with numerous chemical reactions taking place simultaneously.

Cholesterol has several applications and the function it delivers to our body is numerous. It serves as an enzyme synthesizer which is vital for fat metabolism. It is also involved in the creation of estrogen and androgens which are our sex hormones. Cholesterol additionally is a significant component in the creation and maintenance of bodily cells. Cholesterol itself is healthy and is utilized for numerous biological processes.

Because cholesterol is a fatty substance, it cannot be combined with water, just as oil and water cannot. As a result, cholesterol cannot move unhindered through the blood. Therefore, during manufacturing, cholesterol must be joined to particular proteins that serve as "carriers" in the bloodstream. Lipoproteins are created when cholesterol is bound to a protein known as a "carrier". LDL (low-density lipoprotein), also known as "bad cholesterol, and HDL (high-density lipoprotein), also known as "good cholesterol," are two common lipoproteins. A primary kind of LDL is produced by the liver and sent to the body, carrying fatty molecules to all tissues. Since fat is required for all of our cells, this is both healthy and necessary. LDL tends to linger in the bloodstream, which is when it turns into the evil guy. Fat begins to build up in the blood vessels if there is too much of it, forming the atherosclerotic plaque. Paying close attention to LDL levels in the bloodstream is crucial because this is a risk factor for many cardiovascular complications like strokes or heart attacks. However, HDL catches cholesterol in the blood and transports it to the liver, where it is appropriately recycled. Given that HDL prevents cholesterol from harming the cardiovascular system, it stands to reason that we view it as the good guy.

In addition to LDL and HDL cholesterol, there are two more kinds of cholesterol. The next kind is termed "VLDL". This is also termed "extremely low-density lipoproteins". This kind is pretty high when it comes to the number of fats that are contained in it, but quite low when it comes to protein.

The fourth form of cholesterol is termed "triglycerides". Specifically, this particular item is truly a "fat". When an individual encounters VLDL, triglycerides are transported through the blood. This can pose a variety of health problems for an individual

se. If not enough blood and oxygen can reach your heart muscle then chest pains may arise. When your blood flow to the heart is fully stopped this will surely result in a heart attack

The conditions in which our liver produces cholesterol—that is, what occurs inside the body—change how it does so. We produce more cholesterol in the liver when we eat less of it. More cholesterol intake results in the liver producing fewer molecules. This adaptation makes it such that our cholesterol levels don't change all that much. Because of this, foods high in cholesterol including sardines, seafood, cheese, and eggs generally have no effect on a person's blood cholesterol level. However, other processed foods like deep-fried meats, pastries, bacon, sausages, and bacon aren't as safe.

Testing Cholesterol Level

High levels of LDL, IDL, and VLDL lipoproteins lead to a higher risk of a heart attack because these forms of lipoproteins injure arteries. On the other hand, larger levels of HDL lipoproteins minimize the risk of a heart attack because these lipoproteins carry cholesterol away from the bloodstream.

To keep cholesterol at acceptable levels we should focus on lowering LDLs while raising HDLs. This may typically be done by taking care of what sort of food we eat. To determine if we need to manage our cholesterol level we should first measure it. For persons older than 20 years it is advisable to test their cholesterol level every 5 years and adults over 45 years should undergo cholesterol tests every few years.

The level of cholesterol in our blood is evaluated with a blood test. It can be done clinically or at home. There are several home cholesterol test kits available. Some tests evaluate only the total cholesterol level while others can measure additionally HDL and LDL levels. The cholesterol level in our blood is measured in units mmol/l. It is vital to assess both kinds, LDL, and HDL because their ratio is equally significant - the LDL to HDL ratio should be less than 4. Sometimes additionally the Cholesterol/HDL ratio is determined. It is measured by dividing the total cholesterol level by the HDL cholesterol level and for most people, this ratio should be below 5:1. The optimum Cholesterol/HDL ratio is below 3.5:1.

Normal cholesterol levels are the following:
Total cholesterol level: less than 5.5 mmol/l
LDL level: less than 3.5 mmol/l
HDL level: more than 1.0 mmol/l
LDL to HDL ratio: less than 4
Triglycerides level: less than 2.0 mmol/l
Before purchasing in-home cholesterol test kits, we should visit our doctor. Even when cholesterol testing is done by skilled specialists in a lab, there can be substantial variability in test findings. The fluctuation may be considerably bigger with home cholesterol test kits, especially if we're not fasting when we take the test. Home cholesterol test kits are commonly accessible. They are practical, we can quickly estimate our total, HDL, and LDL cholesterol levels in a few minutes. However, we should be also aware of the accuracy of

such home testing. Usually, it is at least 95% but might vary. And we should also remember that home cholesterol testing doesn't replace clinical cholesterol tests - nor do they give a comprehensive evaluation of other risk factors for cardiovascular disease.

Bad Cholesterol

Symptoms of High Cholesterol
Do you wonder what the symptoms of high cholesterol are? Having an increased cholesterol level is not considered an illness, however, it leads to more dangerous problems. Heart attacks and strokes are frequently directly caused by having too much cholesterol.

XANTHELASMA
Finding true signs of an elevated level of cholesterol is quite challenging because none indicate high cholesterol directly. However, in extremely rare situations, you might get something called xanthelasma. If you have xanthelasma, it is completely sure you have an excessive level of cholesterol. Xanthelasma is cholesterol deposits that are visible as yellow spots on the skin. These are frequently placed around the eyes. Having xanthelasma is not common, although it is quite easy to see. Many have tried to surgically remove these patches and failed. Usually, these patches will resurface. It is advisable to avoid xanthelasma in the first place, or rather too much cholesterol in general.

FAMILIAL HYPERCHOLESTEROLEMIA
Familial hypercholesterolemia is another ailment that might signal high cholesterol but it's relatively rare. People with familial hypercholesterolemia, a hereditary condition, can develop cholesterol-containing deposits that can be seen through the skin.
In some of the worst situations, these deposits are disfiguring and might interfere with a person's activities. They are hard yellow nodules that may accumulate on the joints or ligaments.

Sometimes optometrists can notice deposits around the iris or on other areas of the eyes. As people age, optometrists commonly notice drusen in the retina, the light-gathering tissue inside of the eyes. The makeup of the drusen contains proteins and lipids, a portion of which may be cholesterol.

ELEVATED TRIGLYCERIDES
Fats or lipids, proteins, fluids, and nutrients pass from one region of the body to another via the bloodstream. Triglycerides in the circulation comprise a mix of fatty acids and glucose. Levels of triglycerides can become raised when a person eats a high-fat diet.

Elevated triglycerides are a risk factor for illness of the heart and circulatory system. The fatty acids can get oxidized or calcified and create clots. The clots can trigger a stroke or a heart attack.
Since there are few outward signs of high cholesterol, but higher triglyceride levels are considered a risk factor for the development of heart disease, most doctors advise monitoring. The screening includes extracting some blood and submitting it to a laboratory for review.
The laboratory examines the triglyceride and lipoprotein composition of the sample. Lipoproteins are the transport carriers for cholesterols, fatty acids, proteins, and several other nutrients. Lipoproteins are of varied densities. The lower-density molecules have high fat and low protein content. The higher-density ones contain more protein.

ARCUS SENILIS
Arcus senilis is sometimes stated to be one of the signs of excessive cholesterol. It is a gray or white arc or entire circle that develops around the border of the cornea.

The cornea is the transparent lens that covers the outer layer of the eyes. The discoloration is typically noticed in elderly persons and is formed of fat. But, the arcs are not always indicators of high cholesterol or high triglycerides. A blood test is the only way to determine.

When blood levels are proven to be unhealthy, dietary adjustments, exercise, weight loss, avoiding alcohol, or cessation of cigarette smoking are the first suggestions. Doctors often give statin medicines to lower blood levels, if a person is unable to manage the levels on their own.

Alternative practitioners and natural health professionals often propose chemicals found in plants and herbs. Phytosterols, for example, are substances present in soy and other foods that compete with cholesterols for absorption in the digestive tract, which effectively decreases the quantity absorbed.

Since there may be no signs of high cholesterol, high triglycerides, or high blood pressure, yet such things can harm our hearts and brains, it is crucial to have a frequent examinations with your healthcare expert.

Generally, the symptoms of elevated cholesterol are quite infrequent. Usually, elevated cholesterol levels are only diagnosed by blood testing. The bottom line is hypercholesterolemia does not generally present any form of symptoms. The only so-called symptoms are believed to be those displayed as the result of high cholesterol, which is a true health concern such as coronary heart disease, stroke, and peripheral vascular disease.

CORONARY HEART DISEASE
Having any symptom suggesting a high level of cholesterol is exceedingly unusual. Usually, it will not be identified unless you do a blood test. When someone does develop symptoms, the most

prevalent would be angina. Angina is never the same for each individual; experiencing it may consist of mainly chest discomfort, weakness, nausea, perspiration, palpitations, and pain in the arms, neck, or jaw. All of this is an indicator of not enough blood flow to the heart. The blood flow in the veins and arteries is impaired due to the additional cholesterol accumulated in them. Having your blood flow entirely obstructed will result in either a heart attack or stroke.

Angina or chest discomfort is one of the key symptoms that are related to coronary heart disease. When a person is suffering from Angina generally he expresses a sense of "squeezing" or "pressure" in the chest cavity or a general feeling of "someone sitting on their chest". Although the predominant symptom is the sense of pressure in the chest area, these symptoms might move to the jaw, neck, or arm regions of the body. Furthermore, some persons report a sense of pressure in other regions and not the chest.

Other symptoms such as shortness of breath, nausea sweating, lightheadedness, heart palpitations, and dizziness emerge in addition to the stated pressure. Angina should be addressed carefully since it can be directly associated with coronary heart disease. However, eating a heavy meal, a high degree of emotion, and over-exertion can be also deemed to be stressful. You can lessen or even eliminate the symptoms in these conditions by taking a brief time of rest, no more than five minutes or so. Still, rather than thinking that everything is alright if any of these symptoms repeat, it is preferable to consult with your physician.

STROKE
Even though most of the time a stroke is a sudden event with little or no warning at all, there are four basic symptoms linked to a stroke. These are as follows:
- Dizziness, lack of coordination, and loss of balance
- Sudden problem with eyesight in one or possibly both eyes

- Sudden bewilderment. Having trouble in either speaking or comprehending or both
- The abrupt development of numbness or weakness of the face, arm, or leg. This mainly happens on one single side of the body.

There are no indications that imply elevated cholesterol levels, although these are some hints you may follow. If you are unclear or doubting your cholesterol levels, the best and definite thing to do is to have your blood tested. You may ask your doctor to do this test for you. If you have high cholesterol, do not be worried. Knowing you have it is the first step toward change. You will have guidance in your efforts to avoid heart attacks and strokes from happening to you.

Causes of bad cholesterol

Here are reasons Why You May Have High Bad Cholesterol:
1.Genetics
Some genetic variants have been found as being related to high LDL levels, however, these mutations are rare. The disease of familial hypercholesterolemia, for example, is characterized by very high LDL levels, very low HDL (good) cholesterol, and very high total triglycerides. Triglycerides are fats in the bloodstream. High triglycerides are frequently related to high total cholesterol and high LDL.

2. Low HDL Levels
Not only are low HDL levels an accompanying concern linked with high bad cholesterol, but they are also a source of the problem. HDL particles are bigger and more buoyant. They can attract the smaller LDL particles, take them up and bring them back to the liver for refining or elimination. HDL particles are bloodstream scavengers.

3. Diet

Yes, the stuff that you are eating might be driving your levels of cholesterol to soar through the sky. If you are consuming too much-saturated fat in your diet, then your LDL, or bad levels, may be growing. The foods that commonly include these harmful fats include those that come from animals, such as cheeses, milk, pork, butter, eggs, meat, and more. Some packaged foods also are rich in saturated fat. It is essential to adjust the way you eat if your levels are increasing.

Diet can contribute to excessive triglycerides, high total cholesterol, and the imbalance in HDL and LDL particles outlined above. But the cholesterol in your food contributes to just around 20% of the cholesterol circulating in your system. Most of the particles are created by your liver and other physiological organs.

4. Lack of Exercise

Although the relationship between physical inactivity and high bad cholesterol is not entirely understood, it is known that regular physical exercise reduces triglyceride levels and related issues. The most plausible cause is that the muscles consume more fatty acids for sustenance. Triglycerides are made of fatty acids. Another aspect is that muscles utilize fatty acids for nutrition while they are at rest. So, the effects of exercise are long-lasting.

5. Smoking

Smoking adds to elevated bad cholesterol. Nicotine and other substances disrupt the entire circulatory mechanism. Cigarette smoking has a deleterious effect on the liver, where most cholesterol is formed. Your body produces more cholesterol in reaction to cigarette smoking as a supposed defensive mechanism, but the system provides no resistance against the effects of cigarette smoke.

6. Excessive Alcohol Consumption

Cholesterol is a fatty waxy alcohol. Increased alcohol use leads to excessive cholesterol formation.

7. Inefficient Excretion of Cholesterol
Normally, bile acids carry cholesterol out of the bloodstream and out of the body. In some cases, the excretion process is inefficient. This leads to an increased buildup of total cholesterol in the body.

8. Excess Absorption and Reabsorption of Cholesterol
Your body occasionally absorbs more cholesterol than normal from the foods that you eat. Often, this is related to a shortage of other nutrients in the diet. Re-absorption of cholesterol accounts for a substantial percentage of circulating LDL particles. Instead of being expelled by bile acids, the particles are re-absorbed via the intestinal walls.

9. The Role of Oxidation
LDL particles are detrimental because they become caught on the walls of the circulatory system and become hardened via the process of oxidation. So, while balancing and managing cholesterol is vital, it is also necessary to minimize oxidation of the particles, which are generated mostly by free radicals. In my next post, you will discover how to lower bad cholesterol and minimize oxidation, naturally.

Diet and cholesterol
A significant fraction of people (around 40% of the population) are sensitive to some fatty foods. The remaining 60%, however, don't see much of a change in cholesterol response to these items. Therefore, the majority of people are okay with consuming more than two eggs every week. One study found no difference in blood cholesterol levels between persons who consumed four eggs per week and those who consumed one. Therefore, eggs don't seem to

be all that bad. But why do some doctors advise us to consume only a small amount of cholesterol each day?

Some outdated advice was based on research done on rats, who have higher health hazards from dietary cholesterol intake than other animals. Of course, this should worry us. However, the researchers gave these animals an unreasonably excessive amount. Some participants in one trial consumed the daily equivalent of 9500 mg of cholesterol in humans. Who consumes 51 eggs in one day, on average? More recent human research confirm that dietary cholesterol and eggs can be consumed in moderation without damage and have no impact on blood cholesterol levels in the majority of people. I can apparently consume more than two eggs in a week, which is excellent news. While our meals can affect the lipoproteins, or the good and bad cholesterol, that are present in our bloodstream, blood levels of cholesterol do not often change much based on what we consume. But what foods are the best for naturally lowering cholesterol and the worst for high cholesterol?

All are not accepted.

The Mediterranean diet is what makes it all possible, so yes, they could.

The Mediterranean Diet's Natural Cholesterol-Lowering Effects
The prevalence of cardiovascular illnesses is lower among residents of Mediterranean nations. It makes sense that experts would research how the Mediterranean diet affects their bodies because cholesterol is typically associated with heart issues. Researchers examined dozens of papers from earlier decades for a comprehensive study published in 2021. They discovered a pattern: only the Mediterranean diet increases HDL levels, the good cholesterol, while lowering LDL levels, the bad cholesterol, with particular meals. According to research, certain meals like extra

virgin olive oil, tomatoes, almonds, fish, and fish oils have a remarkable effect on HDL and LDL levels in the blood.

Olive oil: Does It Lower Cholesterol?
Fans of the Mediterranean diet frequently use olive oil. However, extra virgin olive oil, which is high in polyphenols, stands out when we're talking about excellent cholesterol. Keep reading even if it might seem like a mouthful. Bioactive compounds or natural chemical molecules fall under the category of polyphenols. Tea, almonds, grapes, avocados, chocolate, and olives are a few examples of plant foods that contain it. These substances support the body's lipid metabolism and offer anti-oxidant protective actions. Researchers observed that patients' HDL cholesterol efflux capacity rose after consuming a Mediterranean diet for a year in a trial involving around 7500 participants. The ability of HDL to esterify cholesterol dramatically improved in the bodies of those who consumed extra virgin olive oil as part of their diet. This indicates that HDL had a greater capacity to transport fat to the liver and remove extra cholesterol from the circulation and blood vessels.

Tomatoes as a Butter Substitute with Olive Oil and Heart Disease
Do tomatoes lower blood cholesterol? Absolutely! Studies have shown that tomatoes, a staple of the Mediterranean diet, have a favorable effect on HDL levels in the blood. In particular, there was some evidence that HDL's metabolism improved dramatically in a trial involving 54 overweight patients who took lycopene, a potent antioxidant present in tomatoes.

Fisheries and fish oils
Omega-3 fatty acids are added to some fish and fish oils (consider salmon, sardines, and oysters). Alpha-linolenic acid (ALA), eicosapentaenoic acid (EPA), and docosahexaenoic acid (DHA), the three major omega-3 fatty acids, have all been linked to lower levels of LDL in the blood. EPA and DHA have been demonstrated to do

this. This is excellent news because patients' risk of cardiovascular disease diminishes when LDL levels in the body are lower.

Cholesterol Reduction Methods

The latest studies demonstrate that, despite what it may seem like, adding extra virgin olive oil, almonds, and fish oils to your diet will improve your heart health in general and that foods high in cholesterol are not always the enemy when it comes to blood cholesterol levels. For my part, I'll continue to cook with extra virgin olive oil in all of my meals and begin consuming more than two eggs this week. Let's see how my subsequent blood test turns out.

7-day Mediterranean diet meal plan

Here's what you can do to get ahead for the week to make your busy weekdays easier. And don't forget to print off the shopping list!

Make 2 servings of Apple-Cinnamon Overnight Oats to enjoy for breakfast on Days 2 and 3.
Prepare Crispy Chickpea Grain Bowl with Lemon Vinaigrette to enjoy for lunch on Days 2 through 5.

Day 1:
Breakfast (279 calories)
- 1 cup nonfat plain Greek yogurt
- 1 small peach, sliced 2 Tbsp. chopped walnuts

A. M Snack (101 calories)
- 1 medium pear

Lunch (360 calories)
- 1 serving of white Bean & veggie Salad

P. M Snack (62 calories)
- 1 cup blackberries

Dinner (405 calories)
- 1 serving sheet-pan chilli-Lime Salmon with Potatoes & Peppers

Daily Totals: 1,208 calories, 74 g protein, 119 g carbs, 32 g fiber, 54 g fat, 7 g saturated fat, 922 mg sodium
Make it 1,500 calories: Add 1 whole-wheat English muffin with 1 Tbsp. natural peanut butter to breakfast and add 1 clementine to lunch.

Make it 2,000 calories: Include all the alterations for the 1,500-calorie day, plus add 1/3 cup unsalted dry-roasted almonds to P.M. snack and add 1 serve Guacamole Chopped Salad to supper.

Day 2:
Breakfast (250 calories)
- 1 serving Apple-Cinnamon Overnight Oats
- 1 clementine

A.M. Snack (37 calories)
- 1 medium bell pepper, sliced

Lunch (370 calories)
- 1 serving Crispy Chickpea Grain Bowl with Lemon Vinaigrette

P.M. Snack (133 calories)
- 1 cup nonfat plain Greek yogurt

Dinner (415 calories)
- 1 serving Spinach Salad with Roasted Sweet Potatoes, White Beans & Basil Vinaigrette

Daily Totals: 1,204 calories, 55 g protein, 150 g carbs, 34 g fiber, 48 g fat, 7 g saturated fat, 1,369 mg sodium

Make it 1,500 calories: Add 1 slice of whole-wheat bread with 1 Tbsp. natural peanut butter and 1/3 cup hummus to A.M. snack.

Make it 2,000 calories: Include all the alterations for the 1,500-calorie day, plus add 1 clementine to lunch, add 1/3 cup unsalted dry-roasted almonds to P.M. snack, and add 1/2 an avocado to supper.

Day 3:
Breakfast (250 calories)
- 1 serving Apple-Cinnamon Overnight Oats
- 1 clementine

A.M. Snack (77 calories)
- 1 tiny apple

Lunch (370 calories)
- 1 serving Crispy Chickpea Grain Bowl with Lemon Vinaigrette

P.M. Snack (8 calories)
- 1/2 cup sliced cucumber
- Pinch of salt & pepper

Dinner (513 calories)
- 1 serving Spiced Grilled Chicken with Cauliflower "Rice" Tabbouleh
- 1 serving Everything Bagel Avocado Toast

Daily Totals: 1,219 calories, 53 g protein, 139 g carbs, 30 g fiber, 54 g fat, 9 g saturated fat, 1,641 mg sodium

Make it 1,500 calories: Add 1 slice of whole-wheat bread with 1 Tbsp. natural peanut butter and 1 medium pear to lunch.

Make it 2,000 calories: Include all the alterations for the 1,500-calorie day, but raise to 2 slices of whole-wheat bread with 2 Tbsp. natural peanut butter for breakfast, add 1/3 cup unsalted dry-roasted almonds to A.M. snack and add 1 medium orange to lunch.

Day 4:

Breakfast (279 calories)
- 1 cup nonfat plain Greek yogurt
- 1 small peach, sliced
- 2 Tbsp. chopped walnuts

A.M. Snack (101 calories)
- 1 medium pear Lunch (370 calories)
- 1 serving Crispy Chickpea Grain Bowl with Lemon Vinaigrette

P.M. Snack (62 calories)
- 1 cup blackberries

Dinner (370 calories)
- 1 serving Sheet-Pan Shrimp & Beets

- 1 serving Basic Quinoa

Daily Totals: 1,182 calories, 74 g protein, 137 g carbs, 31 g fiber, 43 g fat, 6 g saturated fat, 1,255 mg sodium

Make it 1,500 calories: Add 1/3 cup unsalted dry-roasted almonds to A.M. snack and add 1 clementine to lunch.

Make it 2,000 calories: Include all the alterations for the 1,500-calorie day, plus add 1 small apple to breakfast, add 1 whole-wheat English muffin with 2 Tbsp. natural peanut butter to P.M. snack, and raise to 2 servings of Basic Quinoa for dinner.

Meal-Prep Tip: Prepare 3 servings Apple-Cinnamon Overnight Oats to enjoy for breakfast on Days 5 through 7 and soak 1 1/2 cups of dried chickpeas overnight for the Slow-Cooker Mediterranean Chicken & Chickpea Soup. Tomorrow, simmer the soup on Low for 8 hours or on High for 4 hours so it's done in time for supper.

Day 5:

Breakfast (250 calories)
- 1 serving Apple-Cinnamon Overnight Oats
- 1 clementine

A.M. Snack (62 calories)
- 1 medium orange

Lunch (370 calories)
- 1 serving Crispy Chickpea Grain Bowl with Lemon Vinaigrette

P.M. Snack (95 calories)
- 1 medium apple

Dinner (446 calories)
- 1 serving Slow-Cooker Mediterranean Chicken & Chickpea Soup

Daily Totals: 1,223 calories, 54 g protein, 174 g carbs, 36 g fiber, 38 g fat, 7 g saturated fat, 1,482 mg sodium

Make it 1,500 calories: Add 1/3 cup unsalted dry-roasted almonds to A.M. snack.

Make it 2,000 calories: Include all the alterations for the 1,500-calorie day, plus raise to 2 clementines for breakfast, add 2 Tbsp. natural peanut butter to P.M. snack, and add 1 serving Guacamole Chopped Salad to supper.

Meal-Prep Tip: Reserve 2 servings Slow-Cooker Mediterranean Chicken & Chickpea Soup to take for lunch on Days 6 and 7.

Day 6:

Breakfast (250 calories)
- 1 serving Apple-Cinnamon Overnight Oats
- 1 clementine

A.M. Snack (31 calories)
- 1/2 cup blackberries

Lunch (446 calories)
- 1 serving Slow-Cooker Mediterranean Chicken & Chickpea Soup

P.M. Snack (32 calories)
- 1/2 cup raspberries

Dinner (441 calories)
- 1 serving Skillet Lemon Chicken with Spinach
- 1/2 cup cooked brown rice

Daily Totals: 1,200 calories, 70 g protein, 144 g carbs, 33 g fiber, 38 g fat, 8 g saturated fat, 1,526 mg sodium

Make it 1,500 calories: Add 1 whole-wheat English muffin with 1 1/2 Tbsp. natural peanut butter to P.M. snack.

Make it 2,000 calories: Include the change for the 1,500-calorie day, plus add 1/3 cup unsalted dry-roasted almonds to A.M. snack and add 1 medium pear to lunch.

Day 7:

Breakfast (250 calories)

- 1 serving Apple-Cinnamon Overnight Oats
- 1 clementine

A.M. Snack (95 calories)
- 1 medium apple

Lunch (446 calories)
- 1 serving Slow-Cooker Mediterranean Chicken & Chickpea Soup

P.M. Snack (35 calories)
- 1 clementine

Dinner (379 calories)
- 1 serving Whole-Grain Spaghetti with Italian Turkey Sausage, Arugula & Balsamic Tomato Sauce

Daily Totals: 1,205 calories, 64 g protein, 178 g carbohydrates, 33 g fiber, 32 g fat, 6 g saturated fat, 1,476 mg sodium

Make it 1,500 calories: Add 1 whole-wheat English muffin with 1 1/2 Tbsp. natural peanut butter to P.M. snack.

Make it 2,000 calories: Include the change for the 1,500-calorie day, plus add 1/3 cup unsalted dry-roasted almonds to A.M. snack, add 1 big pear to lunch, and add a 1-oz. slice of whole-wheat bread for supper.

Chapter 2

THE MEDITERRANEAN DIET

History of the Mediterranean Diet

In recent years, a rising number of men and women in different nations throughout the world have become increasingly concerned about their health. Because many individuals have grown more worried about their general health, these men and women have paid greater attention to what they consume regularly. In the ultimate analysis, these men and women are adopting dietary selections aimed to improve their general health and welfare.

As individuals have grown more concerned about their health and food, a large number of these same men and women have been interested in the Mediterranean diet regimen. If you are, in reality, a person who understands the link between nutrition and health, you may have a solid interest in the history of the Mediterranean diet regimen.

Before you can correctly comprehend what the Mediterranean diet is all about, you need to appreciate that it is more of a concept than a precise eating routine. In truth, there is no such thing as a Mediterranean diet common to all of the countries in the Mediterranean area of the world. Rather, the "Mediterranean diet" comprises those food products that people who reside in the various nations in the area consume in common.

The Origins of the Mediterranean Diet

The notion of the Mediterranean diet is formed from the eating habits and patterns of the people who occupy the nations of Italy, Greece, Spain, France, Tunisia, Lebanon, and Morocco. As a result, the Mediterranean diet truly comprises a wonderful selection of delightful cuisine. If a person elects to accept the notion of the Mediterranean dining scheme, or if a person elects to follow a Mediterranean diet regimen, he or she will have the capacity to relish a fantastic assortment of delectable cuisine.

The nutrition of the peoples that have colonized the regions around the Mediterranean Sea has stayed practically constant for well over one thousand years. The history of the region is filled with examples of men and women surviving longer than similarly situated individuals who consumed different diets. Through the years, the inhabitants of the Mediterranean Sea region have had longer lives than those in other regions of the world at the same historical time.

At the heart of the Mediterranean diet are foods and drinks that are unique to the geographic region around the Mediterranean Sea. In short, the genesis of the Mediterranean dieting and eating pattern was first created by providence. The residents of the region naturally and reasonably ate those meals and drank those liquids that readily were available in and around their dwellings.

The Historical Elements of the Mediterranean Diet Scheme

As indicated earlier, over the ages, the nutrition of the people of the Mediterranean Sea region has stayed virtually constant. The Mediterranean diet consists of the plentiful eating of a variety of nutritious food products including:
* Fresh fruit
* Fresh veggies
* Low-fat nuts
* Whole grains
* Monounsaturated fat
In a similar line, the Mediterranean diet adopted by people for generation after generation avoids or limits some food products that have been judged detrimental in recent scientific investigations. These less-than-ideal eating products include:

* Saturated fats
* Red and fatty flesh
* Rich dairy products
* Fatty fish

The Historical Effects of the Mediterranean Diet Scheme

As has been alluded to previously in this chapter on the history of the Mediterranean diet regimen, the people who live in the region have a reduced risk of heart disease and related disorders that frequently have a direct nutritional relationship. With the introduction of scientific research that has associated the occurrence of health issues with a bad diet, the good advantages of the Mediterranean diet have been self-obvious.

Research for the past two decades has convincingly proved that the men and women who inhabit the Mediterranean region are plagued with heart disease and comparable disorders significantly less common than those in other regions of the world. The specialists who have done this research have determined that there is a significant chance that the food pattern that is widespread in the Mediterranean area is responsible for sustaining the excellent health of the people who reside in that corner of the world during the past one thousand years.

The Expansive Use of the Historical Mediterranean Diet Scheme

During the past twenty years, a substantial number of individuals in different nations across the world have shifted their attention towards finding healthy diet regimens that are low in saturated fat and that contain plentiful amounts of fresh fruits and veggies. Consequently, the Mediterranean diet has captured the notice of many people who desire to integrate healthy eating into their entire course of cautious living. In brief, the Mediterranean diet contains foods and drinks that, when taken in moderation, can act to minimize the threat of some major diseases and can contribute to developing the required foundation for a long, robust lifespan.

Mediterranean Diet Food Pyramid

For most of us, the most known emblem of a healthy diet is found in the food pyramid. It specifies which foods we should consume in which portion amounts so that our body obtains the nutrients it demands. If you're making a healthy diet plan you would do well to look at the Mediterranean diet food pyramid.

What is the Mediterranean Diet Food Pyramid?
The Mediterranean diet food pyramid is drastically different than the usual one to which we are accustomed. There are several noticeable distinctions, especially;
The Mediterranean one does not have a fats category
Red meat sits at the top of the Mediterranean pyramid as a food to eat least of together with sweets/desserts.
Olive oil is associated with fruit and vegetable as something to be ingested often
The top section of the Mediterranean diet food pyramid starts with red meat as a source of animal protein. Red meat and sweets are the least eaten foods in the Mediterranean, roughly 2-3 times per month. The second group, ingested a couple of times each week, is chicken, eggs, and dairy items like cheese and yogurt. Next comes fish and seafood which are consumed virtually every day. The Mediterranean diet is low in saturated fats and rich in monounsaturated fats and omega 3.
The lowest level of the pyramid is made of fruits, vegetables, legumes (beans), nuts, seeds, herbs, spices, whole grain bread, whole grain pasta, couscous, brown rice, polenta, and other whole grains. People in the Mediterranean rarely eat processed grains (i.e. white flour). A great range of these fresh foods are consumed every day, and they are generally either raw or gently prepared. This signifies that the nutrients are still intact. Cooking meals destroys most nutrients or leaves them indigestible. Hence it is always best to consume food fresh or slightly cooked.

The third leg of the Mediterranean pyramid is the suggestion of six glasses of water per day and a moderate amount of wine (i.e. one glass of red wine with dinner).

It is noteworthy to observe that olive oil is placed alongside the fruit and vegetables in the Mediterranean pyramid. Olive oil is a big element of the Mediterranean diet and many meals incorporate it. Healthful olive oil is extra virgin olive oil.

What to Avoid on the Mediterranean Diet

While the Mediterranean diet is not a rigid diet plan, items that are typically not permitted on the Mediterranean diet include:

- Red meat
- Hot dogs
- Bacon
- Lunch meats
- Sausage
- Heavily processed foods
- Frozen dishes that have a lot of sodium
- Sodas
- Sugary drinks
- Sugary sweets
- Candy
- Processed cheeses
- Refined grains
- White bread
- White pasta
- Products using white flour
- Alcohol (other than red wine)
- Butter Refined, processed, or hydrogenated oils

What Foods Are Allowed on the Mediterranean Diet?

Foods included in the Mediterranean diet include:

- Plant meals that are minimally processed and seasonally fresh Fruits
- Poached or fresh fruit is ideal, which may also be consumed as a dessert
- Vegetables
- Whole grains
- Whole-grain pasta
- Barley Farro
- Couscous
- Bulgur
- Dense, chewy, country-style whole-grain bread loaves without added sugar or butter
- Nuts
- Legumes
- Lentils
- Chickpeas
- Beans
- Peas
- Extra virgin olive oil - This should be the major source of fat
- Cheese (not processed) with low-fat yogurt
- Fresh Fish; avoid fried fish

Chapter 3

10 Low Cholesterol Recipes from the Mediterranean Diet :
Here are 10 Mediterranean dishes that can help decrease your cholesterol and offer you a great lot of joy as well.

1.)Lentil Tabbouleh with Roasted Squash
What is lentil tabbouleh?
Lentil tabbouleh is a version of the tabbouleh with bulgur many of you may be acquainted with. It is excellent for fall and winter as it doesn't rely on tomatoes, but instead concentrates on late-season veggies like butternut squash and peppers. These tend to thrive well over the winter months making this a fantastic lunch on a snowy day.

How can lentils and squash fit into the Mediterranean Diet?
Both lentils and squash are cornerstones of every Mediterranean Diet food plan. Lentils are highly high in polyphenols which have been demonstrated to help lower the risk of heart disease, type 2 diabetes, and maybe cancer while benefitting both the brain and the gut microbiota. Lentils also have one of the highest antioxidant levels compared to other legumes. Butternut squash is also abundant in both polyphenols and antioxidants and its skin has been proven to be useful in decreasing blood glucose. The entire meal is filled with fiber and tons of nutritious benefits.
A quick meal.
The answer to creating this dish lickety-split is to chop the squash thinly and get it in the oven first and then start prepping the tabbouleh. If you are making the lentils at home, start them cooking right away likewise so they have time to cool down. This meal is wonderful served warm or cold. I enjoyed it just a tad on the toasty side.

What is Sumac?

Sumac is a spice that has a strong, acidic taste. It is used largely in middle eastern cookery and is well-recognized as a salad dressing component in Fattoush Salad. Sumac has a distinct flavor, but in this recipe, you may replace paprika if you don't have sumac.

PREP TIME	COOK TIME	TOTAL TIME	COURSE	CUISINE	SERVINGS	CALORIES
15 Minutes	25 Minutes	40 Minutes	Main Course	Spanish	4	451

INGREDIENTS

Squash Prep.

- 1 ripe butternut squash, cut thinly in half-moons
- 1/4 cup extra virgin olive oil
- 2 tbsp maple syrup
- 4 garlic cloves, minced
- 1 tbsp sumac (it adds fantastic flavor, but it may be replaced with paprika for a moderate version) (it offers great taste, but it can be replaced with paprika for a mild version)
- salt & pepper, to taste

Lentil Prep

- 2 cups cooked lentils (canned or made at home with 3/4 cup dry lentils)

Tabbouleh Prep

- 1/4 cup yellow bell pepper, chopped
- 1/4 cup red bell pepper, chopped
- 1/4 cup red onion, chopped

- 1/2 garlic clove, chopped
- 1 lime, juiced 3 tbsp extra virgin olive oil
- 1/2 cup fresh parsley, sliced
- salt, and pepper

INSTRUCTIONS

1. Preheat the oven to 425° F.
2. Line a baking sheet with parchment paper (you may need more than 1 baking sheet) and arrange the squash half-moons. Season them with olive oil, maple syrup, garlic, sumac, salt, and pepper. Roast for 25 minutes, or until golden brown.
3. To create the tabbouleh, combine the lentils, yellow bell pepper, red bell pepper, red onion, garlic clove, lime juice, olive oil, fresh parsley, salt, and pepper.
4. Serve with roasted squash and fresh parsley.

NUTRITION

- Calories: 451kcal
- Monounsaturated Fat: 18g
- Sodium: 15mg
- Potassium: 986mg
- Fiber: 15g
- Sugar: 11g
- Carbohydrates: 50g
- Protein: 12g Fat: 25g
- Saturated Fat: 3g
- Polyunsaturated Fat: 3g
- Vitamin A: 15847IU
- Vitamin C: 77mg
- Calcium: 124mg
- Iron: 5mg

2.) Grilled Salmon Salad with Yogurt Dill Dressing

Grilled Salmon with Yogurt Dill Dressing is incredibly easy to make. There is no marinating needed as the salmon comes out beautifully grilled with only a little spice. I begin by firing up the grill. Whether is charcoal or gas, you want to have well-warmed grates to cook the salmon on.

Grilled Salmon Salad with Yogurt Dill Dressing
Place the salmon filet on a cookie sheet and sprinkle salt and pepper on both sides. Let it sit while you mix the dressing and cut the veggies for the salad which should take around 15 minutes. Once you have the salad ingredients in a bowl and the dressing ready, broil the salmon. Begin grilling with the skin up. Cook on that side for about 5 minutes (I cover the grill if the salmon is too thick to assist the center cook). Then, flip the salmon on the skin side and allow it to finish cooking until the fish begins to flake.
I prefer to enjoy it more on the well-done side, but you may determine how long you want to cook the fish. Top the salad veggies with the heated salmon and then pour over the yogurt dressing. I adore this grilled salmon salad the next day as well!

PREP TIME	COOK TIME	TOTAL TIME	SERVINGS	CALORIES
15 Minutes	15 Minutes	30 Minutes	6	242 Kcal

INGREDIENTS
THE SALMON:
- 1.5 pounds salmon filet
- Salt and pepper
-

THE DRESSING:
- 1/2 cup Greek yogurt
- 1/4 cup chopped fresh dill
- 2 tbsp extra virgin olive oil
- 2 tbsp freshly squeezed lemon juice
- 1 tbsp Dijon mustard
- 2 tsp honey
- 1/8 tsp salt
- 1/4 tsp black pepper
-

THE SALAD:
- 2 cups mesclun salad mix
- 1 cucumber, peeled and sliced 2 carrots, grated 1/4 red onion, chopped into thin rings 2 radishes, sliced thin

INSTRUCTIONS

1. Fire up the grill. Gather all your ingredients
2. Place fish on a baking sheet or big dish. Sprinkle salt and pepper on both sides of the fish. Let sit while making dressing and salad.
3. Whisk all of the salad dressing ingredients in a bowl.
4. In a salad dish or tray that will contain the salmon, add all of the salad veggies.
5. Cook the salmon filet skin side up (if there is skin) first on the grill. Grill for around 5 minutes (time depending on heat and thickness of fish and desired doneness) on one side and then gently turn. Grill on the skin side until done. Remove from the grill
6. Top salad with salmon. Drizzle on the dressing. Serve immediately (however, this salad is just as excellent when the salmon has cooled off as well) (although, this salad is just as good when the salmon has cooled off as well).

NUTRITION
- Calories: 242kcal
- Carbohydrates: 7g
- Protein: 25g
- Fat: 12g
- Saturated Fat: 2g
- Polyunsaturated Fat: 3g
- Monounsaturated Fat: 6g
- Trans Fat: 1g
- Cholesterol: 63mg
- Sodium: 153mg
- Potassium: 770mg
- Fiber: 1g
- Sugar: 4g
- Vitamin A: 3784IU
- Vitamin C: 10mg
- Calcium: 55mg
- Iron: 1mg

3.) Lentil Soup with Olive Oil and Orange (Greek Island of Crete).
This classic Cretan Lentil Soup is a substantial and tasty Mediterranean Diet meal. It's easy to prepare, and you can prep your other ingredients while boiling the lentils. I enjoy cooking this soup on Sunday for weekday lunches. Enjoy with a nice and nutritious chunk of sourdough bread.

PREP TIME	COOK TIME	TOTAL TIME	SERVINGS	CALORIES
10 Minutes	55 Minutes	1 Hour 5 Minutes	6	604 kcal

INGREDIENTS

- 1 pound lentils, cleaned carefully, stones removed
- 6 cups water 1 cup extra virgin olive oil
- 2 cloves garlic, minced
- 2 tbsp. tomato paste
- 1 onion, grated 1 carrot, grated
- 2 orange slices, skin, and meat
- 1 bay leaf
- Salt & pepper, to taste

INSTRUCTIONS

1. In a deep saucepan, add lentils and 6 cups water. Bring to a boil and continue cooking for 15 minutes.
2. Add other ingredients and continue cooking on a low boil for 30 minutes or until the lentils are tender. Add additional water if needed.

NUTRITION

- Calories: 604kcal
- Carbohydrates: 50g
- Protein: 20g
- Fat: 37g
- Saturated Fat: 5g
- Sodium: 64mg
- Potassium: 844 mg
- Fiber: 24g
- Sugar: 4g
- Vitamin A: 1814IU
- Vitamin C: 9mg
- Calcium: 63mg
- Iron: 6mg

4.) Lebanese Hummus (The Best Hummus Recipe)

The range of different varieties of hummus in the grocery store is rising quickly. The issue is, homemade hummus is so affordable and easy to prepare that the store-bought hummus won't taste the same once you sample our version. Hummus is a typical Mediterranean diet dish that is made with extra virgin olive oil, not canola oil, although most store-bought hummus contains canola oil. Your homemade hummus will already taste better and be healthier using extra virgin olive oil.

This hummus contains some garlic but isn't overly garlicky. I also really appreciate the tahini ratio in this recipe because I feel that some hummus has too much tahini which gives a strong aftertaste. The thing that makes hummus so easy to prepare is that you just add all of the ingredients to a food processor and blend it.
I like to use this hummus in a few different ways. I love to dip pita bread in it for a fast snack. I will serve it as an appetizer at lunch or dinner, as it works well with most other Mediterranean diet meals. However, my favorite thing is to make a falafel pita wrap with loads of hummus smeared inside. Here is one of my favorite falafel recipes.

If you're delivering this hummus to a friend's house, dazzle them by garnishing with a drizzle of extra virgin olive oil, a sprinkling of paprika, and a sprinkle of pine nuts. They will be amazed at the appearance as well as the superb Mediterranean flavors of this traditional Lebanese hummus.

PREP TIME	TOTAL TIME	SERVINGS	CALORIES
15 Minutes	15 Minutes	6	152 kcal

INGREDIENTS
- 2-15 ounces cans of chickpeas, drained and rinsed

- 2 cloves garlic, smashed
- 1/4 cup tahini paste
- 1/3 cup freshly squeezed lemon juice
- 1/4 cup extra virgin olive oil
- 1/4 tsp paprika
- 1/2 tsp salt
- 3 tbsp cold water
- pine nuts for garnish (optional).

INSTRUCTIONS
1. Begin by cutting the garlic in the food processor.
2. Add the rest of the ingredients and mix in the food processor until desired consistency.
3. Blend with cold water for a smoother consistency.

NUTRITION
- Calories: 152 kcal
- Carbohydrates: 5g
- Protein: 2g
- Fat: 15g
- Saturated Fat: 2g
- Polyunsaturated Fat: 3g
- Monounsaturated Fat: 9g
- Sodium: 224mg
- Potassium: 78mg
- Fiber: 1g
- Sugar: 1g
- Vitamin A: 15IU
- Vitamin C: 6mg
- Calcium: 20mg
- Iron: 1mg

5.) 30 Minute Baked Turkey Meatballs

These baked turkey meatballs are laden with spices and surprise, mushrooms, to make them a little healthier. I kind of borrowed this recipe from my mom, who reminded me that you can't use enough dry herbs in these turkey meatballs. The first time I cooked these I didn't put nearly enough parsley. I was puzzled why they lacked a little in taste. She understood what she was talking about since they turned out considerably better the second time.

I still wasn't fully satisfied, though. I had used dried basil the first two times since I figured meatballs are Italian, therefore basil should go fine. My third time preparing these I used dried mint instead and it made such a difference. I'm not going to lie, I've never really been a lover of dried basil anyways. I just find it has such a distinct flavor from fresh basil. Trust me, the dried mint works best in these turkey meatballs.

You're probably wondering why I included minced mushrooms in my turkey meatball recipe. Ground turkey is leaner than ground beef so I needed to add extra moisture. The mushrooms add moisture and help hold the meatballs together without needing to use breadcrumbs. Some eggs contribute moisture and help hold them together as well.

There are two keys to this dish. One, create little ping pong-sized meatballs so they cook very rapidly. The beauty of these meatballs is that they're easy to make and quick to cook. Two, baking them at a very high temperature, 425 F to be exact. You shouldn't even need to turn them because they cook rapidly enough.

PREP TIME	COOK TIME	TOTAL TIME	SERVINGS	CALORIES
10 Minutes	15 Minutes	25 Minutes	5	163 kcal

INGREDIENTS

- 1 pound ground turkey
- 1 portobello mushroom or 4 baby bells, finely minced
- 4 cloves garlic, pressed 1 onion, minced
- 1 egg
- 2 tbsp dried parsley
- 1 tbsp dried oregano
- 1 tbsp dried mint
- 1 tsp cumin
- 1/2 tsp salt 1/2 tsp pepper
- 1 tbsp extra virgin olive oil

INSTRUCTIONS

1. Preheat the oven to 425 F.
2. In a mixing dish, add the ground turkey.
3. Add the rest of the ingredients and mix very thoroughly with your hands.
4. Form the meatballs into ping-pong-sized meatballs and put them on an oiled baking pan.
5. Bake for 15 minutes or until the internal temperature of the meatballs is 165 degrees F.

NUTRITION

- Calories: 163kcal
- Carbohydrates: 5g
- Protein: 24g
- Fat: 6g
- Saturated Fat: 1g
- Polyunsaturated Fat: 1g
- Monounsaturated Fat: 3g
- Trans Fat: 1g
- Cholesterol: 83mg
- Sodium: 300mg

- Potassium: 433mg
- Fiber: 1g
- Sugar: 2g
- Vitamin A: 143IU
- Vitamin C: 3mg
- Calcium: 52mg
- Iron: 2mg

6.) Maple Almond Granola with Coconut (Gluten-Free) (Gluten-Free)

Start your morning off right with this delicious, quick & nutritious Granola recipe. This Mediterranean Diet breakfast meal employs a small list of natural foods and has just the perfect touch of sweetness. As a plus, this dish is also gluten-free. Oats are inherently gluten-free, but make sure that your oats are not manufactured in a facility that also processes wheat products.

PREP TIME	COOK TIME	TOTAL TIME	SERVINGS	CALORIES
10 Minutes	1 Hour 15 Minutes	1 Hour 25 Minutes	10	270 kcal

INGREDIENTS
- 3 cups old-fashioned oats (gluten-free) (gluten free)
- 1 cup sliced almonds
- 3/4 cup shredded coconut
- 1/4 cup brown sugar
- 1/4 cup olive oil
- 1/4 cup maple syrup

- 3/4 tsp salt

INSTRUCTIONS
1. Preheat oven to 250 degrees Fahrenheit.
2. In a large mixing basin, whisk together oats, almonds, coconut, and brown sugar.
3. In a small mixing dish, combine olive oil, maple syrup, and salt.
4. Add liquid to dry ingredients. Stir until everything is integrated thoroughly.
5. Spread granola evenly over two cookie sheets. Bake for 1 hour and 15 minutes, stirring every 15 minutes until the granola is golden brown and crispy.

NUTRITION
- Calories: 270 kcal
- Carbohydrates: 32g
- Protein: 5g
- Fat: 14g
- Saturated Fat: 3g
- Polyunsaturated Fat: 2g
- Monounsaturated Fat: 7g
- Trans Fat: 0.002g
- Sodium: 196mg
- Potassium: 204mg
- Fiber: 4g
- Sugar: 14g
- Vitamin A: 0.1IU
- Vitamin C: 0.05mg
- Calcium: 52mg
- Iron: 2mg

7.) Muhammara (Roasted Red Pepper and Walnut Dip)

Something that amazing shouldn't be this easy to create!

The dip may be made from start to finish in 30 minutes. Simply roast the red peppers and walnuts in the oven, put them in a food processor with the rest of the ingredients, and process until smooth and the dip is done. You may serve Muhammara warm or cold and I feel that the tastes are much sharper after being chilled overnight.

I hope you try this spicy, and creamy dip. You will not be disappointed by its drool-worthy taste profile and delicious texture especially when combined with warm pita bread.

PREP TIME	COOK TIME	TOTAL TIME	SERVINGS	CALORIES
10 Minutes	20 Minutes	30 Minutes	2	696 kcal

INGREDIENTS

- 2 roasted red bell peppers
- 1 cup walnuts
- 2 cloves garlic
- 1 tsp pomegranate molasses
- 1/2 lemon juice
- 1 tsp cumin
- 1 pinch crushed red pepper flakes
- 1 tsp salt
- 1/4 cup extra virgin olive oil
- 1/4 cup breadcrumbs

INSTRUCTION

1. Roast bell peppers on a sheet pan for 20 minutes at 400 degrees by breaking them in half and deseeding. Flip once midway. You may toast your walnuts in the oven at the same time by laying walnuts on a sheet pan and allowing roast for approximately 10 minutes (keep an eye on them so as not to let them burn).
2. Put red peppers and walnuts in a blender with the remaining ingredients and mix until smooth and creamy.
3. Garnish with a drizzle of olive oil, a drizzle of pomegranate molasses, and a sprinkle of crushed red or Aleppo pepper.

NUTRITION
- Calories: 696kcal
- Carbohydrates: 22g
- Protein: 11g
- Fat: 66g
- Saturated Fat: 8g
- Polyunsaturated Fat: 31g
- Monounsaturated Fat: 25g
- Sodium: 1773mg
- Potassium: 378mg
- Fiber: 5g
- Sugar: 3g
- Vitamin A: 232IU
- Vitamin C: 22mg
- Calcium: 114mg
- Iron: 4mg.

8.) Mediterranean Fish Stew (30-minute recipe).

Let's set the scene. The toddler is exhausted and wailing. We need to lay her down to sleep in 1 hour which means we have to eat in the next 30 minutes. All we have are some basic veggies; carrots and potatoes; and a pound of halibut. This is my favorite sort of problem to tackle. How to create a tasty supper with what is on hand and do it fast. Mediterranean fish stew is one of those meals: easy (5 minutes of prep, 25 minutes on the burner), wonderful (even our tiny one enjoyed it), and plenty left over for lunch the next day.

I'll be honest, even with my love of anything Mediterranean, I don't prepare fish all that frequently. Generally, I am more likely to acquire fish when I dine out than when I am at home. I adore preparing fish stew though. I had some excellent fish stews when sitting at little tavernas facing the Mediterranean Sea in Crete and I appreciate the simplicity of a few vegetables, fresh herbs or spices, fish, and a decent broth. Plus there was the bonus of seeing the fisherman come in with their haul in the morning and eating it later in the day.

This Mediterranean fish stew is wonderful with any white fish. I have tried it with both halibut and flounder. It is so simple to prepare that even a newbie in the kitchen will find creating it to be a breeze. You don't even have to chop the fish before placing it in the soup because it will break apart naturally on its own.

The easiest side dish to serve the Mediterranean fish stew with is some bread and a Greek salad. We would often have a glass of wine and some tzatziki while we had fish stew on the island.

PREP TIME	COOK TIME	TOTAL TIME	COURSE	CUISINE	SERVINGS	CALORIES
5 Minutes	25 Minutes	30 Minutes	Lunch, Main Course, Soup	Mediterranean	4	391 kcal

INGREDIENTS

- 2 tbsp butter
- 2 tbsp extra virgin olive oil
- 1 onion, chopped
- 1 carrot, cut into thin rounds
- 1 tbsp flour
- 3 medium potatoes, peeled and chopped into bite-sized pieces
- 1 pound white fish (cod, halibut, haddock) boneless
- 4 cups chicken broth, reduced sodium or normal
- 1/2 tsp smoked paprika
- Salt & pepper, to taste

INSTRUCTIONS

1. Heat butter and olive oil in a heavy-bottomed saucepan. Sauté onions and carrots until tender (approximately 3 minutes). Stir in flour and then add potatoes. Cook on medium heat for 1 minute.
2. Add chicken broth and bring to a boil. Add fish and smoked paprika. Cover and boil, stirring periodically until potatoes are cooked (approximately 15-20 minutes) (about 15-20 minutes). Fish should flake into little bits.

NUTRITION

- Calories: 391 kcal
- Carbohydrates: 36g
- Protein: 29g
- Fat: 15g
- Saturated Fat: 5g
- Polyunsaturated Fat: 2g
- Monounsaturated Fat: 7g
- Trans Fat: 1g
- Cholesterol: 64mg
- Sodium: 204mg

- Potassium: 1442mg
- Fiber: 5g
- Sugar: 3g
- Vitamin A: 2895 IU
- Vitamin C: 36mg
- Calcium: 61mg
- Iron: 2mg

9.) Bean Burgers with Garlic and Sage

A really good bean burger recipe is hard to find. I have tried hundreds of them over the years and this Mediterranean Diet based bean burger recipe is one of my all-time favorites.

Bean Burger Recipe with Garlic and Sage

There are a few things that make this bean burger recipe so good.

Eggs – Many bean burgers fall apart, but the addition of eggs makes it so it stays together as a burger throughout the frying.

Garbanzo Bean Flour – This also helps to bind the burger and adds flavor. It also makes the burger gluten-free (you could use regular flour or bread crumbs, but I recommend the Garbanzo Bean Flour if you can find it.

Fried in Olive Oil – Frying the bean burgers in healthy olive oil adds flavor, but more importantly, it creates an almost crispy outer layer. As you probably know, you can safely fry with olive oil on medium heat. You just don't want the oil to smoke (it can steam, but not smoke).

Garlic and Sage – Garlic and sage give the bean burger a sausage-like flavor that I love.

Mediterranean Diet Recipe: Bean Burger with Garlic and Sage

Bean burgers are super quick and great to make when you don't know what you are making for lunch or dinner. Just grab the ingredients from the pantry, prepare (10 minutes), fry (10 minutes) and within 20 minutes your meal is ready.

Condiments are always vitally important for any burger, but I love them on bean burgers! Dijon mustard, catsup, mayo, relish, sauerkraut, lettuce, tomatoes, and onion slices are just a few possibilities for burger night.

If you are going on a super traditional burger night, you could make sweet potato fries and roasted cauliflower. Bean burgers also go well with a salad like our avocado, radish, and cucumber salad or fried onion salad with black olives.

PREP TIME	COOK TIME	TOTAL TIME	SERVINGS	CALORIES
10 Minutes	10 Minutes	20 Minutes	5	305 kcal

INGREDIENTS

- 1-29 ounces can of pink beans, rinsed and drained
- 1/2 onion minced
- 2 eggs
- 1 cup parsley, chopped
- 3/4 cup chickpea flour
- 1/2 tsp black pepper
- 1/2 tsp dried sage
- 1 tsp salt
- 1 tsp oregano, dried
- 2 cloves garlic, minced or pressed
- 1/2 cup Olive oil to fry

INSTRUCTIONS

1. In a bowl, mash beans with a fork. Mash well, but don't puree. I usually stop mashing when beans can be easily formed into a ball without falling apart.
2. Add all other ingredients (except olive oil). Blend well with a fork.
3. Heat oil on medium heat. Form bean mixture into patties. Fry until golden brown on one side and then flip and fry the same on the other side. Drain on paper towels.

NUTRITION
- Calories: 305 kcal
- Carbohydrates: 14g
- Protein: 7g
- Fat: 25g
- Saturated Fat: 4g
- Polyunsaturated Fat: 3g
- Monounsaturated Fat: 17g
- Trans Fat: 1g
- Cholesterol: 65mg
- Sodium: 510mg
- Potassium: 295mg
- Fiber: 3g
- Sugar: 3g
- Vitamin A: 1122IU
- Vitamin C: 17mg
- Calcium: 49mg
- Iron: 2mg.

10.) Avocado Toast with Caramelized Balsamic Onions

We have been compiling an outstanding collection of avocado toast recipes over the last several weeks. There have been a few flops, but mainly they have come out wonderful. When I resided on the Greek island of Crete, one of my favorite culinary experiences was eating fresh avocado from the patio of our hotel. Nothing beats a perfectly ripe avocado whether you are in the Mediterranean or California. This is a very tasty avocado toast dish. It's vegan and quite satisfying and the fat from the avocado and extra virgin olive oil makes for a rich flavor. The sweetness of the caramelized onions creates a lovely balance with the acidity of the balsamic vinegar. A recommendation for this is to find decent bread. I recommend locating a local bakery. Some of my favorite kinds of bread for avocado toast include sourdough, baguette, focaccia, olive bread, and fresh Italian bread.

The avocado is a robust superfood that is abundant in healthy monounsaturated fats (which are also high in extra virgin olive oil), antioxidants, fiber, and other anti-inflammatory components. Avocados may lower cholesterol, and triglycerides and lessen the risk of cancer.

I adore this as a replacement for eggs in the morning. If I have an early avocado toast, I am generally content until lunchtime and I feel fantastic throughout the morning. Of course, you don't have to have this only for breakfast, avocado toast makes a fantastic lunch as well. If you are cooking it at work, you will want to wait to cut the avocado until you are ready to eat. Avocado doesn't preserve that well unless it is combined with an acid like lemon juice. Caramelize the onions in the morning and then bring everything to work and make your co-workers envious! Enjoy this and our other avocado toast recipes!

PREP TIME	COOK TIME	TOTAL TIME	SERVINGS	CALORIES
5 Minutes	20 Minutes	25 Minutes	2	503 kcal

INGREDIENTS

- 1/4 cup extra virgin olive oil
- 1 onion, sliced salt, and pepper, to taste
- 1 tsp dried oregano
- 2 tbsp Balsamic vinegar
- 1 ripe avocado
- 2 pieces toast

INSTRUCTIONS

1. Heat the olive oil over medium heat. Add the onions, salt, and pepper. Saute for about 20 minutes, stirring periodically, until caramelized.
2. Add the balsamic vinegar to the onions and simmer for 2 minutes. Remove from the heat.
3. In a bowl, mash the avocado, oregano, and a bit more salt and pepper, using a fork until smooth.
4. Toast your 2 pieces of bread. Top with avocado mixture. Top this with caramelized onions and enjoy!

NUTRITION

- Calories: 503 kcal
- Carbohydrates: 29g
- Protein: 5g
- Fat: 43g
- Saturated Fat: 6g
- Polyunsaturated Fat: 5g
- Monounsaturated Fat: 30g
- Cholesterol: 1mg
- Sodium: 144mg
- Potassium: 627 mg
- Fiber: 9g
- Sugar: 6g
- Vitamin A: 165IU
- Vitamin C: 14mg

- Calcium: 71mg
- Iron: 2mg.

Chapter 4

10 Mediterranean Diet Breakfast Recipes

1.)Pan con Tomate

The pan con tomate is based on an old custom in Cataluña. Originally called as "pa amb tomaquet", the Catalonian ritual was to take stale bread and massage it with raw garlic and slices of tomato, then spray it with olive oil and sprinkle it generously with salt. It is a fantastic way to take advantage of day-old bread. It continues to be made this way all across Cataluna and many areas in Spain.

The first time I experienced this delightful tapa was on a beach in Calafell, Tarragona in Cataluña, with my friend Beth who had offered me to stay with her family for a week. On my first night there, as the sun sank, we cooked the tostas along with family and friends to complement a magnificent BBQ with grilled sardines, chorizo, zucchini, and peppers. I was in paradise. It was only the beginning of a fantastic stay with friendly chats over one fresh, wholesome, beautifully prepared dinner after another.

I now create pan con tomate by mixing raw tomatoes, olive oil, salt, and, if preferred, a half clove of garlic in the blender. I prefer to sprinkle additional oil on the bread first and follow with a substantial amount of tomato mixture and just a little salt. This is my son's favorite breakfast whenever he comes to visit. He puts a small piece of Jamon serrano (or even better Iberico) on top and loves it with his coffee. Whenever my parents would arrive from the States for a visit I would have it ready along with freshly squeezed orange juice. So basic yet everyone's favorite.

The tostas are not only good for breakfast but may be cooked as tapas before lunch or dinner, or can stand alone as a modest late meal or Cena. The choices are unlimited with tostas con tomate, since you may top them with nutritious combinations of smoked salmon, anchovies, sardines, tuna, eggplant, avocado, manchego, blue cheese, or whatever sounds delicious to you.

PREP TIME	TOTAL TIME	COURSE	CUISINE	SERVINGS	CALORIES
10 Minutes	10 Minutes	Breakfast	Spanish	4	153 kcal

INGREDIENTS
- 1/2 baguette, sliced into 1" circles
- 1 clove garlic
- 1 medium ripe tomato
- 2 tbsp extra virgin olive oil pinch of salt

INSTRUCTIONS
1. Crush garlic on the skin with a knife to remove the peel. Cut a ripe tomato in half. Add garlic, tomato, 2 Tablespoons olive oil, and a sprinkle of salt to a blender. Puree till smooth.
2. Toast baguette slices in an oven (broil) or toaster oven.
3. Drizzle a little olive oil on each slice of bread and then top with a tablespoon of the tomato sauce.
4. Top with Jamon Iberico, Jamon Serrano, Prosciutto, or tuna or salmon.

NUTRITION
- Calories: 153 kcal

- Carbohydrates: 17g
- Protein: 3g
- Fat: 8g
- Saturated Fat: 1g
- Polyunsaturated Fat: 1g
- Monounsaturated Fat: 5g
- Sodium: 193mg
- Potassium: 110mg
- Fiber: 1g
- Sugar: 1g
- Vitamin A: 256IU
- Vitamin C: 4mg
- Calcium: 29mg
- Iron: 1mg

2.) Blueberry Overnight Oats with Greek Yogurt

Breakfast is done when you wake up. I am not the sort of person who eats the same thing for breakfast every day for my whole life. I enjoy variety, but it drives me a bit crazy when I get up in the morning and I can't figure out what I want to eat. Blueberry overnight oats are a terrific approach to fix this problem because it is already there waiting for you when you first open the fridge. There is something fantastic about having a convenient meal that you created yourself.

What are Overnight Oats?
While overnight oats have been all the craze for the last several years, there are still many who haven't tried them and don't realize how easy they are to cook. I have become a more recent convert myself. The original overnight oats were only oats and milk with cinnamon, but they have grown into a much broader pallet of tastes. This blueberry overnight oats dish includes, besides oats and blueberries, Greek yogurt, almond milk, vanilla, cinnamon, maple

syrup, walnuts, and chia seeds. The chia seeds, when they soak in almond milk, provide a pudding-like texture and the walnuts give it a delicious crunch. I have always appreciated anything with the combination of blueberries and maple syrup, such as my recipe for blueberry compote, and they don't disappoint here. The primary idea of overnight oats is that with no cooking you will get a wonderful dessert like breakfast with only 5 minutes of prep. It is, in fact, a lazy cook's fantasy.

Are Overnight Oats Healthy?

If done with care, overnight oats are one of the most nutritious meals out there. It is vegetarian, gluten-free, and follows the rules of the Mediterranean Diet. Besides being satisfying, it also pretty low in calories and heavy in fat which is a fantastic mix for weight reduction. Blueberries are one of the greatest antioxidant foods. Walnuts and Chia seeds are both filled with omega-3 fats, polyunsaturated fat that most of us are lacking, and aid with anything from melancholy and anxiety to heart disease and inflammation. Oats, likewise highly abundant in antioxidants, help lower cholesterol and improve blood sugar. So, sure, overnight oats are healthy.

How Long Do Overnight Oats Last?

If you cooked overnight oats at the beginning of the week I would attempt to consume them before the end of the week. I feel these taste best when eaten 1 or 2 days after you make them. You may wait longer, but, after time it won't taste as fresh and lively.

What Kind of Oats for Overnight Oats?

You can use practically any sort of oats for overnight oats, but you don't want to use fast oats. Old-fashioned rolled oats are the finest. If you are gluten-free, you do want to make sure the oats you are using come from a gluten-free facility (the container should mention this) (and the package should say this).

How to Make Blueberry Overnight Oats

These are the easiest breakfast recipe out there (save for pouring milk over cereal) (except for putting milk on cereal). All you have to do is mix all the ingredients (except the walnuts) into a bowl, cover, and refrigerate. The next morning you will have breakfast prepared for you. Top with nuts and enjoy!

PREP TIME	TOTAL TIME	COURSE	CUISINE	SERVINGS	CALORIES
5 Minutes	5 Minutes	Breakfast	Mediterranean	2	270 kcal

INGREDIENTS
- 1/2 cup rolled oats
- 1/3 cup plain greek yogurt
- 2/3 cup unsweetened almond milk
- 1 tsp vanilla extract
- 1/2 tsp cinnamon
- 1-2 tsp maple syrup dash of salt
- 1/2 cup frozen or fresh blueberries
- 1/4 cup toasted walnuts
- 1 tbsp chia seeds

INSTRUCTIONS
1. Add all ingredients except walnuts into a bowl. Cover and refrigerate overnight.
2. Serve topped with toasted walnuts.

NUTRITION
- Calories: 270 kcal
- Carbohydrates: 28g

- Protein: 10g
- Fat: 14g
- Saturated Fat: 1g
- Polyunsaturated Fat: 9g
- Monounsaturated Fat: 2g
- Trans Fat: 1g
- Cholesterol: 2mg
- Sodium: 124mg
- Potassium: 251mg
- Fiber: 6g
- Sugar: 8g
- Vitamin A: 29IU
- Vitamin C: 4mg
- Calcium: 211mg
- Iron: 2mg

3.) Buckwheat Pancakes with Coconut Cream

I wake up every once in a while with a strong hankering for pancakes. The trouble with my pancake cravings is that they used to wreck my whole day. When I would prepare ordinary pancakes with white flour and sugar I would feel tired and mopey for the rest of the day. My stomach would feel bloated and I would get acidic (sometimes needing to take an antacid) (sometimes needing to take an antacid). If you are going to eat pancakes, buckwheat is the way to go. This pancake is still fluffy and full of the flavor that comes with the coconut cream, vanilla, and maple syrup. Top them with your favorite toppings. You will find my recommendations below.

Why should I consume buckwheat?
Unlike many other flours, buckwheat is considered a low glycemic index meal. It is considerably better for your blood sugar than white or even wheat flour and helps to avoid undesired blood sugar rises.

Buckwheat flour is also filled with fiber, protein, and loads of anti-oxidants. It is a fantastic vegetarian source of protein.

Don't let the term buckwheat mislead you.... It's gluten-free! Buckwheat is a funny name for something that isn't wheat at all. Buckwheat is naturally gluten-free.

Where can I purchase buckwheat flour?

Buckwheat flour is accessible in the bread area of most stores. I obtain organic buckwheat flour in bulk at our local co-op. Not only is it organic, but it is quite a deal less expensive because it comes in quantity. You can also purchase online at Amazon, but it looks to be quite a deal less expensive if you can find it in a store.

How do I preserve buckwheat flour?

If you are using it fast, simply keep it in a cold, dark spot. If you are intending to just use it infrequently you should store it in the freezer (I put it in freezer bags or a mason jar) (I put it in freezer bags or a mason jar). It should last up to 6 months in the freezer.

Ten Minutes of Prep and Breakfast is on its way.

Buckwheat pancakes are incredibly easy to prepare. Mix dry ingredients. Whisk wet ingredients. Add dry ingredients to wet ingredients. Mix lightly and you are good to go. I usually always use extra virgin olive oil when I prepare pancakes or crepes. You want to make sure that you cook the pancakes on a low enough heat so the olive oil doesn't smoke. Medium heat is typically fine.

7 options for buckwheat pancakes
1. Add 1 peeled and sliced apple to the batter. Sprinkle with cinnamon.
2. Top with your homemade blueberry syrup (cook 1 cup blueberries and 1/4 cup maple syrup on low heat until syrup develops a beautiful purple hue.)
3. Add a sliced banana to the batter. Top with syrup and walnuts.
4. Top with sliced peaches and crème Fraiche.

5. Add 1 cup of blueberries to the batter.
6. Top with bananas, chocolate chips, and whipped cream.
7. Topp with strawberry syrup (cook 1 cup sliced strawberries with 1/4 cup maple syrup over low heat until syrup is warm.

PREP TIME	COOK TIME	TOTAL TIME	COURSE	CUISINE	SERVINGS	CALORIES
10 Minutes	20 Minutes	30 Minutes	Breakfast	Mediterranean	2	572 kcal

INGREDIENTS
- 2/3 cup buckwheat flour
- 1 teaspoon baking powder
- 1/4 teaspoon baking soda
- 1/4 teaspoon salt 1 egg
- 1/4 cup coconut cream
- 3/4 cup almond milk or whole milk
- 1 teaspoon vanilla
- 2 tablespoons maple syrup
- 4 teaspoons extra virgin olive oil

Topping:
- 1/2 cup full-fat yogurt
- 1/4 cup maple syrup

INSTRUCTIONS
1. Mix dry ingredients (buckwheat flour, baking powder, baking soda, and salt) in a bowl with a fork.
2. Whisk wet ingredients (egg, coconut cream, almond milk, vanilla, and 2 tablespoons maple syrup) in another bowl.

3. Add dry ingredients to wet ingredients. Mix with a spoon (don't overmix).
4. Fry pancakes in a skillet with olive oil (2 teaspoons per round of pancakes.) Flip once bubbles develop throughout the pancake.
5. Top with a dollop of yogurt and a Tablespoon of maple syrup.

NUTRITION
- Calories: 572 kcal
- Carbohydrates: 90g
- Protein: 10g Fat: 20g
- Saturated Fat: 9g
- Polyunsaturated Fat: 2g
- Monounsaturated Fat: 8g
- Cholesterol: 90mg
- Sodium: 727mg
- Potassium: 466mg
- Fiber: 5g
- Sugar: 58g
- Vitamin A: 179IU
- Vitamin C: 1mg
- Calcium: 272mg
- Iron: 2mg

4.) Sweet Potato Hash with Eggs
Breakfast will never be the same. This recipe for Sweet Potato Hash with Eggs is very quick, tasty, and sure to leave you pleased, and ready to start the day.

This rethinking of hash makes it an excellent morning choice. We replaced normal potatoes with sweet potatoes, which means extra vitamin A, antioxidants, and potassium. We also took out processed meats and, instead, incorporated uncured chicken sausage into the recipe to assure the exquisite meaty qualities while feeling confident in the integrity of the meat.

A key part of why this sweet potato hash dish is a healthier alternative to typical hash is that it is plant-based instead than animal-based. The trick is picking plant-based foods that will provide a comparable feeling to consuming something animal-based. That's why we picked mushrooms and red peppers in this dish as our supplementary veggies.

As always, we cooked our hash in extra virgin olive oil. Extra virgin olive oil is one of the finest fats since it is filled with antioxidants, is little processed, and is used by people who demonstrate the lowest rates of heart disease in the world (Crete!). Here is great research on the relationship between olive oil intake and heart disease if you are interested in knowing more!

Another amazing part of this sweet potato hash dish is that it's completely done and ready to go on a single sheet pan. Sheet pan recipes are fantastic because they make cooking easy, enable the tastes of all the components to come together, and streamline the clean-up afterward. Not to add, the appearance of the completed meal is amazing. This sweet potato hash is no exception. So, next time you desire a plentiful breakfast that won't leave you feeling too stuffed and weary, check out this dish.

PREP TIME	COOK TIME	TOTAL TIME	COURSE	CUISINE	SERVINGS	CALORIES
15 Minutes	35 Minutes	50 Minutes	Breakfast, Lunch	Mediterranean	4	486 kcal

INGREDIENTS

- 2 sweet potatoes peeled and sliced into little ½ inch cubes
- 3 tablespoons extra virgin olive oil divided
- 1 teaspoon smoked paprika
- ½ teaspoon salt
- ½ teaspoon pepper
- 2 medium onions cut into ½ inch cubes
- 2 uncured pre-cooked sausages of your choosing (I like spicy chicken) (I like spicy chicken)
- 1 red pepper cut into ½ inch pieces
- 6 baby portobello mushrooms sliced into ½ inch slices
- 1 Tablespoon balsamic vinegar
- 8 eggs

INSTRUCTIONS

1. Preheat oven to 400 degrees F.
2. Spread sliced potatoes equally on a sheet pan. Add 2 Tablespoons olive oil, smoked paprika, salt, and pepper. Stir potatoes until they are well covered with oil and seasonings.
3. Bake in the oven for 10 minutes.
4. Remove from oven and add onions, sausages, red pepper, and mushrooms. Drizzle on another tablespoon of olive oil with a tablespoon of balsamic vinegar. Mix well, ensuring sure all veggies are coated properly.
5. Bake in the oven for 20 more minutes or until vegetables are browned.

Remove from oven. Crack eggs on top of vegetables and potatoes.

6. Bake for 5 more minutes or until the eggs are done.

NUTRITION

- Calories: 486kcal
- Carbohydrates: 32g
- Protein: 21g

- Fat: 30g
- Saturated Fat: 8g
- Polyunsaturated Fat: 4g
- Monounsaturated Fat: 16g
- Trans Fat: 1g
- Cholesterol: 358mg
- Sodium: 755mg
- Potassium: 847mg
- Fiber: 5g
- Sugar: 10g
- Vitamin A: 17719IU
- Vitamin C: 45mg
- Calcium: 106mg
- Iron: 3mg

5.) Greek Omelette with Zucchini and Mint (Crete)

Ever since I started cooking, I have always been trying out different recipes since I adore producing something new and wonderful. This recipe for a Greek omelette with zucchini and mint is one of those meals that fills me with delight. I shall always think of that first time I cooked it for my father. Since that day, I've cooked it often.

Zucchini has been one of my favorite veggies since childhood. Growing up, my family cultivated numerous veggies in our garden and every spring I would wait and watch till the first zucchini started to sprout. I recall thinking how lovely it was that our garden was loaded with veggies and herbs that would ultimately become ingredients for dishes.

On one occasion, I wanted to surprise my dad by preparing him an omelette. I went to the garden and selected the first zucchini that was growing. I cleaned it, sliced it, and then put salt on it, placing it in a strainer to drain. Then I went back out to the garden and gathered fresh mint and got fresh eggs from our birds. From there, I created the omelette, and both my dad and I enjoyed it.

PREP TIME	COOK TIME	COURSE	CUISINE	SERVINGS	CALORIES
5 Minutes	10 Minutes	Breakfast, Lunch	Crete, Greek	4	333 kcal

INGREDIENTS
- 2 tiny or 1 large zucchini
- 4 eggs
- 2 Tablespoons extra virgin olive oil
- Salt and pepper to taste
- 5 leaves fresh mint, chopped ¼ cup feta cheese

INSTRUCTIONS
1. Fry lightly salted zucchini slices in olive oil till golden on all sides. Remove the zucchini with a fork and set it on a paper towel (reserving the olive oil in the pan).
2. Beat the eggs with salt, pepper, and mint.
3. Heat reserved oil, and add eggs. Spoon zucchini onto one side of the eggs. Flip to make an omelet. Serve with Greek feta cheese.

NUTRITION
- Calories: 333kcal
- Carbohydrates: 8g
- Protein: 16g
- Fat: 27g
- Saturated Fat: 7g
- Polyunsaturated Fat: 3g
- Monounsaturated Fat: 14g

- Trans Fat: 0.04g
- Cholesterol: 344mg
- Sodium: 355mg
- Potassium: 646mg
- Fiber: 2g
- Sugar: 5g
- Vitamin A: 962IU
- Vitamin C: 35mg
- Calcium: 175mg
- Iron: 3mg

6.) Spinach and Goat Cheese Quiche (France)

You surely remember the renowned French dish: Quiche Lorraine. It is a blend between a frittata and a savory tart. It's loved in France, it's really simple to create and you can use your leftovers to make it. It is often eaten for supper at home or lunch at local eateries and bakeries. In America, it would usually be served at brunch or as a morning quiche.

Instead of the ham and shredded cheese of the original Quiche Lorraine, this variation is prepared with spinach and goat cheese, so it's a vegetarian dish and a bit healthier.

About the cheese, it's fairly usual to obtain fresh goat cheese in France, it is liked with a slice of bread. In America, I can't get some at Walmart but you can have some at Wegmans, Whole Food, or Trader Joe's. My favorite is the Fresh Goat Cheese I find at Trader Joe's. It is nice and not too pricey. In France, there are thousands of various shapes for goat cheese, in the form of a log, circular, or even square. They also have various maturity, some are more full-bodied since they have slept longer but for this dish, fresh is ideal. Moreover, for the moment, I have discovered only extremely fresh goat cheese in the shape of a log.

Finally, the spinach, There is enormous spinach in France and French people need to remove the spinach tails. Here, I find fresh spinach and it's easy. No need to peel them you can just fry them in the skillet.

I hope you will appreciate this excellent French morning quiche recipe. Serve with a salad and a slice of bread. Don't forget, you may construct your Quiche variant with all the components you like. You simply need to preserve these ingredients: eggs, half and half, sour cream, and the pie crust, of course!

PREP TIME	COOK TIME	TOTAL TIME	SERVINGS	CALORIES
10 Minutes	45 Minutes	55 Minutes	4	352 kcal

INGREDIENTS
- 1 frozen pie crust
- 3 eggs
- 1/2 cup half and half
- 3 tbsp sour cream
- 10 ounces of fresh spinach
- 6 slices fresh goat cheese (about 2 ounces)
- 1/2 tbsp
- 1/4 tsp black pepper

INSTRUCTIONS
1. Remove the crust from the freezer and let it defrost as you prepare the remainder of the ingredients.
2. Preheat the oven to 390°F.

3. Chop spinach into tiny pieces. Cook them in a pan with up to 1/4 cup water. Cook until spinach is wilted. Drain water and squeeze out any excess liquid from the spinach.
4. In a medium-sized bowl, beat the eggs and then add half & half, sour cream, salt, and pepper. Whisk until smooth. Add the spinach and stir with a spatula or spoon.
5. Pour the egg mixture into the pie crust. Top with pieces of goat cheese.
6. Bake for roughly 45 minutes or until the quiche has set.

NUTRITION
- Calories: 352kcal
- Carbohydrates: 25g
- Protein: 13g
- Fat: 23g
- Saturated Fat: 10g
- Polyunsaturated Fat: 2g
- Monounsaturated Fat: 9g
- Trans Fat: 1g
- Cholesterol: 145mg
- Sodium: 639mg
- Potassium: 540mg
- Fiber: 3g
- Sugar: 1g
- Vitamin A: 7135IU
- Vitamin C: 20mg
- Calcium: 159mg
- Iron: 4mg

7.) Spinach and Ricotta Frittata (Southern Italy)
Although not typically encountered in restaurants, in Italy frittata is a relatively common meal to create at home. It's a typical party starter or a terrific picnic dish, but you can surely eat it at any time of the day you like, from breakfast to dinner.

The most classic frittata variants are the ones cooked with zucchini or onions. However, you may truly use any vegetable that you prefer and adjust this dish to your unique taste. In reality, most Italian home chefs create this meal with leftover greens or with whatever they have on hand. You can technically create a frittata with anything, but the only item you can't ignore is cheese.

Frittata is a really simple egg-based meal, incredibly quick to prepare and rapid to bring together. Even more, it's excellent both hot and at room temperature. I think this may be an excellent recipe for those parents who would like to persuade their kids to eat more vegetables without conflict.

As I was saying, there are limitless frittata varieties, but this specific one is probably in the top 5 of my favorites. It asks for a lot of fresh spinach is wonderful for your health, and the ricotta cheese makes it softer and much more pleasant. If you want to make this a complete dinner, you could combine this spinach and ricotta frittata with a lovely seasonal salad.

Prep notes:
The final step to prepare any Italian frittata is to complete the classical flip-over, generally with the aid of the lid or with a big serving dish. However, if you don't feel confident enough or the pan is too heavy, you may always complete the cooking under the broiler for 2 to 3 minutes. In this situation, just be sure you use a frying pan that is oven safe.
Enjoy!

PREP TIME	COOK TIME	TOTAL TIME	SERVINGS	CALORIES
10	20	30	4	277 kcal

Minutes	Minutes	Minutes		

INGREDIENTS

- 1 big onion, thinly sliced
- 3 tbsp extra virgin olive oil
- 1 pound spinach, large stems removed salt and pepper, to taste freshly ground nutmeg, to taste (just a dash)
- 4 eggs
- 1/4 cup Parmesan cheese, grated
- 1/2 cup ricotta cheese

INSTRUCTIONS

1. Heat a large pan over medium heat and sprinkle the bottom with 2 tablespoons of olive oil.
2. Add onion and sautée for 8 to 10 minutes until the slices get tender and transparent.
3. Then, add spinach straight from the box. Stir for a few more minutes until the leaves are thoroughly wilted.
4. When the onions and spinach are done, sprinkle with salt and freshly ground nutmeg.
5. Meanwhile, in a large bowl, mix eggs with a touch of salt and pepper. Stir in Ricotta cheese and Parmesan cheese.
6. Add the greens to the egg and cheese mixture and whisk everything together.
7. Drizzle some more extra virgin olive oil (about 1 Tablespoon) into the same pan you have used to sauté the veggies. This step is necessary to avoid sticking.
8. Turn the heat on low and pour everything back in. Make sure the bottom of the pan is fully coated and that the contents are evenly spread.
9. Cover with a cover and cook for roughly 10 minutes, until the egg on top is starting to set and the bottom is lovely and hard.

10. Finally, turn the frittata with the aid of the cover and cook it for 5 more minutes so that the opposite side also becomes browned.
11. Serve hot or at room temperature.

NUTRITION
- Calories: 277kcal
- Carbohydrates: 9g
- Protein: 15g
- Fat: 21g
- Saturated Fat: 7g
- Polyunsaturated Fat: 2g
- Monounsaturated Fat: 11g
- Trans Fat: 1g
- Cholesterol: 185mg
- Sodium: 275mg
- Potassium: 788mg
- Fiber: 3g
- Sugar: 2g
- Vitamin A: 11063IU
- Vitamin C: 35mg
- Calcium: 279mg
- Iron: 4mg

8.) Traditional Italian Biscotti (Cantucci Toscani)

Cantucci, sometimes called Biscotti di Prato, is a classical sweet dessert from northern Tuscany. They have a very old history and are today regarded as the most traditional dessert in the whole region. Imagine that the earliest formal record of their existence comes from a book written in 1691!

These cookies are frequently offered after the meal combined with Vin Santo, a Tuscan dessert wine produced from raisins that were originally used to celebrate Mass. Of course, you may opt to eat them with coffee, tea, or milk or just enjoy them on their own!

The name biscotti technically means twice (bis) cooked (cotto) and in reality, Cantucci, is the icon of twice-baked cookies. They are really simple to prepare, you simply have to mix all the ingredients, form the dough into long logs, and bake them. Then, when the logs are still warm, cut them into slices and fry them again.

Once made, you may preserve cantucci in a sealed container for several weeks, and have one once in a while as a treat. At my house, though, they barely ever stay for more than a few days, especially around Christmas!

Prep notes:

This is the most classical Cantucci recipe, and it asks for raw unpeeled almonds. However, if you'd prefer to have a different filling, you can easily substitute the almonds with other kinds of nuts or anything else you want, from dried fruit to dark chocolate chips. That said, I'd encourage you to sample the original version first: it's excellent!

Finally, according to tradition, these cookies should be fairly firm and dry as they are generally dipped in sweet wine. Nevertheless, if you like your cantucci to be a bit softer, all you have to do is to lower the second baking time by a few minutes.

PREP TIME	COOK TIME	TOTAL TIME	SERVINGS	CALORIES
15 Minutes	30 Minutes	45 minutes	18	190 kcal

INGREDIENTS

- 1 cup unpeeled almonds
- 1 1/4 cup sugar
- 3 eggs, plus 1 for brushing
- 1 tbsp honey
- 3 cups all-purpose flour
- 1 tsp baking powder
- 1 orange zest 1 pinch salt

INSTRUCTIONS

1. Preheat oven to 370 F.
2. Roughly cut half of the almonds.
3. In a large bowl, add sugar, honey, and eggs. Whisk for a couple of minutes until the compound gets lighter in color.
4. Add flour, baking powder, orange zest, and salt. Mix everything until fully blended.
5. When you get a crumbly texture, add the almonds, both chopped and whole.
6. Shape the dough into three long logs (approximately 1 1/2 inches high) and set them on the baking sheet, coated with parchment paper. Remember to leave enough space between the logs to allow for rising.
7. Evenly brush the log's surface with an egg.
8. Bake for 20 minutes, until golden brown.
9. Take the logs out of the oven and decrease the temperature to 330 F.
10. Cut the logs diagonally into 1/2-inch pieces using a serrated knife.
11. Put the slices back onto the baking tray, and cut the sides down. Cook for another 8 to 10 minutes.

NUTRITION
- Calories: 190kcal
- Carbohydrates: 33g
- Protein: 5g

- Fat: 5g
- Saturated Fat: 1g
- Polyunsaturated Fat: 1g
- Monounsaturated Fat: 3g
- Trans Fat: 1g
- Cholesterol: 27mg
- Sodium: 37mg
- Potassium: 91mg
- Fiber: 2g
- Sugar: 15g
- Vitamin A: 42IU
- Vitamin C: 1mg
- Calcium: 43mg
- Iron: 1mg

9.) Harcha (Moroccan Semolina Biscuits).

Harcha, or Moroccan Semolina Biscuits, are particularly popular in Morocco and are eaten commonly on Sundays as well as for breakfast or kaskrout (afternoon tea time). They can be eaten with sweet or savory meals and occasionally are packed with veggies. I prefer them on their own or with honey and perhaps some cream cheese. Harcha is a hearty snack as well as it may also be served as a biscuit with soup or salad for lunch. It reminds me of an extremely excellent southern U.S. biscuit with a fresh, bright flavor since it utilizes semolina flour instead of white flour. Semolina is abundant in protein and iron and has a far lower glycemic index than white or wheat bread (semolina flour =44, whole wheat flour = 69, white flour = 85). In other words, it will have a significantly better influence on your blood sugar than conventional white or wheat bread.

The nicest thing is how easy these are to create. Add the dry ingredients to a food processor or blender, pulse on high for 30 seconds, and then pour in the olive oil and then the water. You want the final result to be the consistency of thick hummus. It should end up taking about 5 minutes to create the dough. Then you let it soak for 10 minutes to half an hour and you are ready to cook in the skillet.

The last step in creating harcha is molding each biscuit with your hands (you can alternatively use a round biscuit or cookie cutter to cut uniform shapes) and then heating them in a pan. You want each side to be browned up without scorching them. I prefer to fry them on medium heat. Some people add a small amount of olive oil to the pan which will make the semolina biscuits a little crisper, but I like to do it without any oil.

PREP TIME	COOK TIME	TOTAL TIME	SERVINGS	CALORIES
5 Minutes	15 Minutes	20 Minutes	6 Thick Biscuits or 10 Flat	360 kcal

INGREDIENTS
- 2 cups fine semolina
- 1 tsp baking powder
- 1/2 tsp salt 1/2 cup extra virgin olive oil
- 1/2-1 cup water

INSTRUCTIONS
1. Add the semolina, baking powder, and salt to a food processor or blender. Mix until combined.
2. Slowly sprinkle in olive oil while the food processor is on low. With the food processor running on low, slowly trickle in water just until the mixture goes from chunky to a smooth dough. Turn off as soon as dough consistency is attained. Let the mixture rest for half an hour.

3. Let the mixture settle for at least 10 minutes and up to 30 minutes.
4. Make patties from the dough, roughly the height and breadth of an English muffin.
5. Heat a skillet on low-medium. Add the patties and cook on each side until browned (approximately 5 minutes on each side).

NUTRITION
- Calories: 360kcal
- Carbohydrates: 41g
- Protein: 7g
- Fat: 19g
- Saturated Fat: 3g
- Polyunsaturated Fat: 2g
- Monounsaturated Fat: 13g
- Sodium: 266mg
- Potassium: 104mg
- Fiber: 2g
- Calcium: 50mg
- Iron: 3mg

10.) Avocado Toast with Smoked Salmon, Fresh Dill, and Caper
Gourmet has never been as simple as this Avocado Toast with Smoked Salmon, Fresh Dill, and Capers! This is the ultimate combination of flavors: salty capers and smoked salmon, acidic lemon juice, and the crispy bite of red onions coupled with creamy avocado and toasty crusty bread. This takes approximately 10 minutes to cook and is excellent on the weekend when there is time to fully taste the flavor. It is my favorite avocado toast recipe!

How to Make Avocado Toast?

It's incredibly easy! Just open up a ripe avocado and remove the pit. My favorite technique for eradicating the pit is utilizing this procedure:

After removing the pit from the avocado, scoop it out into a bowl and throw in freshly squeezed lemon juice and salt. Lemon and avocado have complementing tastes that are only improved with a small bit of salt (Mediterranean sea salt is best). And voilà! You have the base of your avocado flavor. But, the greatest part is yet to come.

Show Stopping Toppings

When it comes to avocado toast, proper toppings are crucial. This recipe asks for smoked salmon, capers, onion, and fresh dill, which will lift your toast to the next level. Despite this dish being so sweet, you might be shocked to find that each slice contains just 200 calories! It's abundant in good fats so it will also fill you up and fuel you up. Not to add, smoked salmon is abundant in Omega 3 fatty acids, which have been found to support a healthy body on the cellular level.

PREP TIME	TOTAL TIME	SERVINGS	CALORIES
10 Minutes	10 Minutes	2	199 kcal

INGREDIENTS
- 1 ripe avocado
- 1/2 lemon juice
- Dash of salt
- 2 ounces smoked salmon, thinly sliced
- A few tiny stalks of fresh dill
- 10 capers

- A couple of small pieces of red onion
- 2 big slices of bread or 4 little slices of bread

INSTRUCTIONS

1. Cut the avocado in half, and remove pit. Scoop out flesh and mash with a splash of salt and lemon juice.
2. Toast bread. Spread avocado on bread. Top with capers.
3. Top avocado and capers with a slice or two of smoky salmon and then with dill and red onion pieces. Serve immediately.

NUTRITION

- Calories: 199kcal
- Carbohydrates: 10g
- Protein: 7g
- Fat: 16g
- Saturated Fat: 2g
- Polyunsaturated Fat: 2g
- Monounsaturated Fat: 10g
- Cholesterol: 7mg
- Sodium: 304mg
- Potassium: 548mg
- Fiber: 7g
- Sugar: 1g
- Vitamin A: 175IU
- Vitamin C: 13mg
- Calcium: 18mg
- Iron: 1mg

Chapter 5

Mediterranean Snack Recipes

When you're following the Mediterranean diet plan, you don't have to worry about giving up snacks. Mediterranean, who eat naturally and regionally like snacks just like you do. The trick is to stay with the plan's principles and consume what is fresh and good for you. These countries have a climate that supplies them with excellent, ripe fruits and veggies all year round. A lot of snacks also focus on nuts and seeds, which are high in calories, but also beneficial for your metabolism and your heart. These Mediterranean snack recipes will give you a series of go-to delights that won't knock you off course.

Feta Hummus

Store-bought hummus doesn't even come close. Keep this nutty dip available for when you feel like munching on cucumbers, carrots, or pita.

Makes 12 servings

INGREDIENTS
- 1½ cups dry chickpeas
- 1 tsp. baking soda
- 3 garlic cloves, diced
- ½ cup tahini
- ⅓ cup lemon juice (adjust for taste)
- 1 tsp. salt
- ⅓ cup olive oil
- ⅓ cup feta cheese crumbled
- 2 tbsp. chopped parsley

INSTRUCTIONS

1. Place the chickpeas in a bowl of water and refrigerate overnight.
2. In a large pot, combine the chickpeas and baking soda and cook for 3 minutes while stirring.
3. Pour in 8 cups of water and bring to a boil.
4. Lower the heat and add the garlic. Let simmer for about 1 hour.
5. Drain all of the water except for ¼ cup.
6. Place the chickpeas in a bowl filled with water and agitate to help loosen their skins. Use a slotted spoon to discard skins.
7. Drain the chickpeas and place them in a food processor. Purée until smooth.
8. While pureeing, add in the ¼ cup reserved water, tahini, lemon juice, and salt.
9. Once blended, transfer the hummus to a bowl and refrigerate for one hour.
10. When you are ready to use the hummus, adjust the seasoning and drizzle with the oil.
11. Top with the feta and parsley.

Nutrition Facts (Per Serving) Calories: 212 Fat: 13.4 g Sat Fat: 2.4 g Carbohydrates: 17.9 g Fiber: 5.4 g Sugar: 3.1 g Protein: 7.2 g Sodium: 364 mg

Caprese Kebobs
Few things are as abundant in the Mediterranean as tomatoes. Put them to good use with this simple snack.

Makes 3 servings

INGREDIENTS

- 15 grape tomatoes
- ½ cup mozzarella cheese, cut into cubes
- 3 fresh basil leaves
- 1 tbsp. olive oil
- 1 tbsp. balsamic vinegar
- Sprinkle of sea salt
- Black pepper
- 3 kebab spears

INSTRUCTIONS
1. Divide the grape tomatoes and the mozzarella cubes into three piles. Place a tomato, then a bit of cheese on each spear until you have used up your ingredients.
2. One basil leaf should also go on each kebob.
3. Drizzle with oil and vinegar and sprinkle with salt and pepper.

Nutrition Facts (Per Serving) Calories: 165 Fat: 6.7 g Sat Fat: 1.3 g Carbohydrates: 24.2 g Fiber: 7.4 g Sugar: 16.2 g Protein: 6.8 g Sodium: 59 mg.

Spicy Olives
You'll love snacking on these seasoned olives.

Makes 8 servings

INGREDIENTS
- 2 tsp. coriander seeds
- ½ cup olive oil
- 4 pieces orange zest
- 2 tsp. chopped garlic clove
- 2 cups olives
- 1 tbsp. ouzo

INSTRUCTIONS

1. Crush the coriander seeds with a mortar and pestle.
2. Place them in a small pan and whisk while cooking for one minute.
3. Add the olive oil and the rest of the spices and stir for another minute.
4. Add the olives and the ouzo and heat until the olives are warmed.
5. Strain the mixture into a basin.
6. If wanted, use some crusty bread to dip in the oil.

Nutrition Facts (Per Serving) Calories: 148 Fat: 16.2 g Sat Fat: 2.3 g Carbohydrates: 2.4 g Fiber: 1.1 g Sugar: 0 g Protein: 0.3 g Sodium: 293 mg

Roasted Eggplant Dip
Be sure to obtain eggplants when they're in season. They make a terrific healthful snack.

Makes 4 servings

INGREDIENTS

- 1 eggplant
- ¼ cup olive oil
- ½ cup feta cheese
- ½ cup red onion, chopped 2 tbsp.
- lemon juice
- 1 bell pepper, diced
- 1 tbsp. chopped basil
- Salt and pepper to taste

INSTRUCTIONS

1. Preheat the broiler. The rack should be 6–7 inches from the heat.
2. Cover a baking pan with aluminum foil and arrange the eggplant on top.
3. Broil for around 18–20 minutes, flipping it 3 times. Let the eggplant cool 4. Place the lemon juice in a small bowl.
4. Cut the eggplant open and scoop the flesh out. Add flesh to the lemon juice and coat. Pour in the olive oil and whisk.
5. Add the other ingredients and combine well.
6. Serve with fresh vegetables or pita chips.

Nutrition Facts (Per Serving) Calories: 203 Fat: 17 g Sat Fat: 4.7 g Carbohydrates: 11.3 g Fiber: 4.8 g Sugar: 6.5 g Protein: 4.3 g

Spiced Nuts

If you're someone who wants a crunch with your munching habit, these hot and flavorful nuts will satisfy your demand.

Makes 20 servings

INGREDIENTS

- 1 cup almonds
- 1 cup walnuts
- 1 cup cashew and cup peanuts
- ¼ tsp. cayenne pepper
- ½ tsp. red pepper flakes
- ¼ tsp. chili powder
- 1 tbsp. olive oil
- ½ cup raisins

INSTRUCTIONS

1. Preheat the oven to 375 degrees F.

2. In a bowl, mix all the nuts with olive oil and spices. Toss with your hands until everything is coated.
3. Layer the nuts onto a baking sheet and roast in the oven for 20–30 minutes.
4. Remove the nuts and allow them to cool for about 5 minutes. Then, put them back into the bowl and stir them with the raisins.

Nutrition Facts (PerServing) Calories: 164 Fat: 13.6 g Sat Fat: 1.6 g Carbohydrates: 8 g Fiber: 2 g Sugar: 3.1 g Protein: 5.6 g Sodium: 3 mg

Fruity Nut Bars
Makes 24 bars

INGREDIENTS
- ½ cup quinoa flour
- ½ cup oats
- ¼ cup flax meal
- ¼ cup wheat germ
- ¼ cup chopped almonds
- ¼ cup dried apricots
- ¼ cup dried figs
- ¼ cup honey tbsp. cornstarch

INSTRUCTIONS
1. Preheat the oven to 300 degrees F.
2. In a large bowl, combine all ingredients and stir thoroughly.
3. Spread mixture in a half an inch-thick layer in a parchment-lined sheet pan and bake for 20 minutes.
4. Let cool and cut.

Nutrition Facts (Per Bar) Calories: 53.8 Fat: 1.3 g Sat Fat: 0.1 g Carbohydrates: 9.7 g Fiber: 1.4 g Sugar: 4.7 g Protein: 1.4 g Sodium: 1.4 mg.

Chapter 6

10 Mediterranean Diet Lunch ideas and Recipes
1.)Tuna Patties Fried in Olive Oil (France).

These little French tuna patties are fast to make and use just ingredients that you probably already have. Don't worry if you have most of the ingredients, but are missing one or two. These patties adapt to what you have, especially with herbs. If you don't have parsley, but you do have dill then use dill. If you don't have shallots, add onions. Tuna patties work with plenty of different components.

Everyone will adore them
Tuna patties are the perfect dish for an everyday living since it is relatively economical yet tastes so fantastic. The French are beginning to cut their meat consumption and are seeking vegetables or fish-based alternatives to consume at lunch or in the evening. This is why tuna patties are a typical meal that we adore. It is also wonderful for youngsters since they adore this healthier version of a fish stick. You may also create this dish using them. You have to put your "hand to the dough" as the French say and it amuses them a lot.

What to serve with tuna patties
To serve, nothing extra is necessary with this dish. If you want to eat light, pair them with veggies or salad. It will be the perfect cool summer supper. You can also make them a little thicker and put them between two salad leaves, tomatoes and onions and eat them like a light burger. Do not hesitate to prepare homemade tzatziki to accompany them, it goes really nicely or just top with plain yogurt or sour cream. Finally, for the nights with summer friends, form these patties into little balls and bake them in the oven, they will be crispy and delightful dipped in a creamy sauce.

PREP TIME	COOK TIME	TOTAL TIME	SERVINGS	CALORIES
10 Minutes	15 Minutes	25 Minutes	4	215 kcal

INGREDIENTS

- 2-7 ounces cans of tuna
- 1/3 cup bread crumbs
- 2 shallots, chopped 1 tbsp parsley, chopped 3 tbsp chives, chopped 1 tbsp scallions, chopped 1/3 cup parmesan, grated 1/3 cup all-purpose flour + 2 Tablespoons
- 1 tbsp sour cream
- 1 egg
- Salt & pepper, to taste
- 2 tbsp extra virgin olive oil

INSTRUCTIONS

1. Drain the tuna and throw it in a bowl, add all the ingredients except the 2 tbsp of flour and the olive oil. Mix thoroughly.
2. Place the 2 Tablespoons of flour on a small dish. Form medium patties set them in the flour and cover them lightly with it.
3. Heat a frying pan on medium heat and add the olive oil. Cook the burgers for about 7 minutes on each side until gently golden.

NUTRITION

- Calories: 215kcal
- Carbohydrates: 17g
- Protein: 10g

- Fat: 12g
- Saturated Fat: 3g
- Polyunsaturated Fat: 1g
- Monounsaturated Fat: 6g
- Trans Fat: 1g
- Cholesterol: 55mg
- Sodium: 249mg
- Potassium: 142mg
- Fiber: 1g
- Sugar: 2g
- Vitamin A: 356IU
- Vitamin C: 4mg
- Calcium: 132mg
- Iron: 2mg

2.)Pesto Genovese (Traditional Italian Pesto)

In principle, authentic pesto Genovese should be created entirely using a marble mortar and a wooden pestle. Nowadays. however, these time-honored instruments have become more and more commonly merely elegant adornment and a means to commemorate our past culinary customs. Today, the overwhelming majority of home chefs create pesto with the aid of a compact food processor.

In fact, with just a few methods, you can produce a wonderful pesto sauce in less than 10 minutes. That said, if you have a mortar and pestle and some time to spare, you can attempt this recipe with the more conventional approach, the sauce will simply come out a bit chunkier. If you use a food processor, the only thing you have to keep in mind is not to over-process the sauce. To accomplish so, all you have to do is to pulse lightly and in an intermittent method.

Finally, although this dish is produced with just a handful of components, the golden guideline to get a fantastic outcome is to utilize high-quality raw materials: young and brilliant green

Genovese basil (sweet basil) is an absolute requirement, as well as superb extra virgin olive oil.

This pesto sauce may be stored in the refrigerator for a few days in an airtight container and it also freezes extremely nicely. The most typical method to eat it is with Trofie pasta, cooked together with a few potatoes and some green beans. However, there are limitless dishes that incorporate it as a primary element!

Enjoy!

Prep notes: This original recipe asks for a tiny bit of Pecorino Sardo, a pungent sheep cheese made in Sardinia. If you are not able to purchase it at your local supermarket, you may replace it with any other Pecorino cheese or you can just increase the amount of Parmesan cheese. If this is the case, however, you may want to modify the amount of salt proportionally as Pecorino Sardo is sweeter than typical old Pecorino cheese.

PREP TIME	TOTAL TIME	SERVINGS	CALORIES
10 Minutes	10 Minutes	8	222 kcal

INGREDIENTS

- 3.5 ounces Genovese basil leaves (sweet basil)
- 1 cup Parmesan cheese
- 1/4 cup Pecorino Sardo cheese
- 1/3 cup pine nuts
- 1 clove garlic
- 1/2 tsp coarse sea salt
- 1/2 cup extra virgin olive oil (plus 1 tbsp to put on top)

INSTRUCTIONS

1. Gently wash basil leaves under cold water and drain them completely until they are quite dry.
2. In a food processor, combine Parmesan cheese, Pecorino Sardo cheese, pine nuts, and garlic.
3. Add basil leaves and salt.
4. Continue to mix until you get a smooth consistency, carefully dripping the olive oil on top of the other ingredients during the process. Be cautious not to over-blend the sauce or the blades will start to burn the basil.
5. Finally, pour the pesto into a jar and top it with little extra olive oil to minimize oxidation.

NUTRITION
- Calories: 222kcal
- Carbohydrates: 2g
- Protein: 7g
- Fat: 22g
- Saturated Fat: 5g
- Polyunsaturated Fat: 3g
- Monounsaturated Fat: 12g
- Cholesterol: 12mg
- Sodium: 384mg
- Potassium: 86mg
- Fiber: 1g
- Sugar: 1g
- Vitamin A: 767IU
- Vitamin C: 2mg
- Calcium: 205mg
- Iron: 1mg

3.) Authentic Greek Salad (Horiátiki Salata)

In 2014, I visited Greece for the first time and enjoyed my first Authentic Greek Salad. I had waited my entire life to eat true Greek cuisine. I was also hoping to compile some true Mediterranean Diet dishes.

I landed in Athens and was scheduled to go on a study tour across the nation. I went to my hotel and the study group was waiting for me to go to dinner together. I deposited my baggage in my room and we proceeded across the crowded streets to a classic Greek taverna. The server gave us bread with extra virgin olive oil to dip. The oil was very amazing. Then he delivered the greek salad. This was a moment I will never forget. I took one mouthful of a crimson, juicy tomato slice and I thought to myself "What have I been eating my whole life?!" This was the sweetest, most tasty, deep crimson, and meaty tomato I had ever sunk my teeth into.

Then I tasted the feta…. I genuinely questioned the other students if we got the salad with goat cheese instead of feta. They laughed at me and said no, this is what the feta is like in Greece. I was in heaven only one hour into my journey. I began to ponder again what feta had I been eating all these years that I thought was so good. There's something that happens with a true Greek salad. The tomatoes contain so much liquid, that by the time the salad is mostly finished, the oil, tomato juice, feta, onion, and oregano have produced this delicious dipping sauce.

Anyone who has eaten a real Horiatiki Salata knows that this is the absolute tastiest and healthiest juice to dip your bread in. I could eat this salad twice a day daily, and we did it on this study tour. The salads were even tastier the farther out of the city and into the countryside we ventured. To me, this is the finest salad in the world. A summer supper without this salad just isn't happening.

PREP TIME	COOK	TOTAL	COURSE	CUISINE	SERVINGS	CALORIE

	TIME	TIME				S
10 Minut es	0 minute s	10 Minut es	Main Course , Salad	Crete, Greek	2	546 kcal

INGREDIENTS
- 3 medium tomatoes, quartered
- 1 big cucumber, peeled and sliced
- 1/4 red onion, sliced into strips
- 1/4 red bell pepper, sliced into thin strips
- 10 kalamata olives
- 6 ounces of feta cheese
- 1/4 cup extra virgin olive oil
- 1 splash of red wine vinegar or lemon juice
- 1/2 tsp oregano salt and pepper, to taste

INSTRUCTIONS
1. Add all veggies and olives to a bowl.
2. Top with feta cheese, olive oil, lemon juice (or vinegar), and oregano. Salt and pepper, to taste.

NUTRITION
- Calories: 546kcal
- Carbohydrates: 17g
- Protein: 15g
- Fat: 48g
- Saturated Fat: 17g
- Cholesterol: 76mg
- Sodium: 1173mg
- Potassium: 734mg
- Fiber: 4g

- Sugar: 12g
- Vitamin A: 2059IU
- Vitamin C: 32mg
- Calcium: 479mg
- Iron: 2mg

4.) Avocado Toast with Smoked Salmon, Fresh Dill, and Capers:
Procedures can be found in page

5.) Moroccan Harira (Lentil and Chickpea Soup)
This is the account of how Harira is produced in Morocco by Hajiba (Mahjouba Ezzamoury) as translated by her daughter-in-law, Hannah Holz.

Harira is one of the most characteristic and famous soups in Morocco. Hajiba makes it at least once a week and they would eat it largely for supper, but it's also a delicious breakfast.

Since she was a tiny kid, Hajiba used to help her parents to prepare Harira.

Nowadays Hajibas Mum, who happily lives in the same area, sometimes comes around to Hajibas' home to make Harira together. It became kind of their routine whenever both have the time.

So as Hajiba starts by removing the skin of the tomatoes, her mom cleans cilantro, parsley, and celery.

The sliced onion, half of the greens, and all of the tomatoes go into a blender to be combined.

Then Hajiba chooses a huge pot because they generally cook a significant amount of soup for a couple of days. She pours the combined concoction into this saucepan with roughly half a liter of water. Now she sets it on a high burner at the beginning and her mom and she starts to add all the spices including knorr (or the substitute) and olive oil. Also, the lentils are included. They'll let it stew for a bit and utilize the opportunity to relay the current news. It's usually a wonderful moment for them anytime they get the

92

chance to cook together, so laughter can be heard throughout the whole home.

After roughly 10 minutes, Hajiba adds the pasta and chickpeas. She also adds between 1 – 1 ½ liters of water. Meanwhile, her mom puts flour and some more water in the blender until it has a smooth texture. Then she stirs it into the soup.

In the end, Hajiba adds the tomato paste and the remainder of the sliced greens and lets it boil for a little while longer. If you desire different consistency just add additional water to the soup until you like it. Also, you may add some extra salt or other spices if needed. When everything is soft, they prefer to serve Harira with bread, dates, or figs. Also, a dash of fresh lemon juice complements it quite nicely.

Enjoy!!

PREP TIME	COOK TIME	TOTAL TIME	SERVINGS	CALORIES
10 Minutes	30 Minutes	40 Minutes	6	194 kcal

INGREDIENTS
- 1 big onion
- 1/2 bunch cilantro (approximately a cup, lightly packed), rinsed, big stems removed
- 1/2 bunch parsley (approximately a cup, loosely packed), rinsed, big stems removed
- 1 stick celery, finely chopped
- 4 tomatoes, skins removed
- 1/2 cup dry green lentils, washed and checked for stones
- 1 tsp salt 1 tsp powdered pepper 1 tsp turmeric
- 1/2 tsp ginger

- 1/2 piece of any salted vegetable bouillon cube
- 2 tbsp extra virgin olive oil
- 4 tbsp tomato paste
- 1 cup cooked (canned) chickpeas
- 1/2 cup (2 ounces) fine pasta (angel hair), broken in quarters
- 2 tbsp all-purpose white flour

INSTRUCTIONS

1. Add onion, half of the cilantro, and half of the parsley, celery, and tomatoes to a blender or food processor. Blend until smooth.
2. Add pureed veggies and 2 cups of water to a large soup pot. Bring to a boil over high heat and then add the lentils, salt, pepper, turmeric, ginger, bouillon cube, olive oil, and tomato paste. Bring to a boil again and then simmer on a low boil for 10 minutes.
3. After 10 minutes, add chickpeas, pasta, and 4 cups of water. Bring to a boil and simmer for 5 minutes while you create the flour/water combination.
4. In a blender or food processor, combine 1/4 cup flour and 1/4 cup water until smooth. Slowly add the flour-water mixture to the soup. Simmer for 5 more minutes.
5. Add the remainder of the chopped herbs, and boil for a few minutes. Salt & pepper, to taste.

NUTRITION

- Calories: 194kcal
- Carbohydrates: 28g
- Protein: 8g
- Fat: 6g
- Saturated Fat: 1g
- Polyunsaturated Fat: 1g
- Monounsaturated Fat: 4g

- Sodium: 620mg
- Potassium: 609mg
- Fiber: 9g
- Sugar: 5g
- Vitamin A: 1333IU
- Vitamin C: 23mg
- Calcium: 50mg
- Iron: 3mg

6.) Grilled Cheese with Feta and Sun-Dried Tomatoes

It is the end of summer, but we are still enjoying fresh food and the taste of garden-grown tomatoes. However, with the onset of the winter, I also want some warm cuisine. This nutritious grilled cheese is the perfect lunch for that! Good ingredients are crucial to prepare this healthy grilled cheese. You need decent-grade feta cheese. This cheese does not truly melt but it combines extremely well with the other elements. By the way, because we appreciate the "melted" cheese in this hot sandwich, I decided to put some finely shredded mozzarella cheese. The combination of these two kinds of cheese is wonderful and tasty.

Now let's add some freshness. Adding salad may sound unusual but it's wonderful for the final flavor! I adore incorporating greens in my dish, it's nutritious and fresh. My favorite is arugula, really yummy. But you may also select spinach or any sort of salad. Last but not least: sun-dried tomatoes! This item adds zing, you don't need plenty of them to have a pleasant flavor. In addition, don't add too many sun-dried tomatoes or it won't be wonderful.
This feta grilled cheese is fantastic with a delicious gazpacho, a cold soup with tomatoes, cucumber, and bell peppers. If you are in a fall/winter mood, select a hot tomato soup, the combination with sun-dried tomatoes is excellent. This is also really great with a simple salad, like an actual Greek salad.

I truly hope you will love my fresh feta grilled cheese! Don't forget to pick wonderful ingredients! You can make simple cuisine spectacular with properly pick components.

PREP TIME	COOK TIME	TOTAL TIME	SERVINGS	CALORIES
5 Minutes	10 Minutes	15 Minutes	2	514 kcal

INGREDIENTS
- 3 tbsp extra virgin olive oil
- 4 slices whole grain bread
- 1/2 cup finely shredded mozzarella cheese
- 1/3 cup feta cheese
- 1/4 cup sun-dried tomatoes, chopped
- 2 tiny handfuls of arugula

INSTRUCTIONS
1. Brush one side of each slice of bread with olive oil (using all 3 Tablespoons of oil). Place each slice of bread oil side down.
2. On one piece of bread, put half of the mozzarella, half the feta (slightly crumbled), half the tomatoes, and half the arugula. Cover with a slice of bread. Repeat to construct the second sandwich.
3. Heat a skillet (non-stick or cast iron) to medium heat. Add sandwiches and fry on one side until golden brown (approximately 4-5 minutes). Flip and cook 2nd side until golden brown. Eat immediately!

NUTRITION

- Calories: 514kcal
- Carbohydrates: 33g
- Protein: 19g
- Fat: 35g
- Saturated Fat: 11g
- Polyunsaturated Fat: 3g
- Monounsaturated Fat: 19g
- Cholesterol: 44mg
- Sodium: 718mg
- Potassium: 721mg
- Fiber: 6g
- Sugar: 10g
- Vitamin A: 891IU
- Vitamin C: 8mg
- Calcium: 372mg
- Iron: 3mg

7.) Beet and Carrot Salad with Toasted Walnuts and Goat Cheese

You can't top this beet recipe! This is a savory, well-rounded and crisp salad to illustrate how wonderful and attractive your winter veggies can be. Use our recipe for dijon vinaigrette.

How to toast walnuts: Toast walnuts in a pan over medium-high heat for 3-5 minutes, turning regularly. Be cautious not to burn!

PREP TIME	TOTAL TIME	SERVINGS	CALORIES
15 Minutes	15 Minutes	4	275 kcal

INGREDIENTS

- 4 cups lettuce

- 2 carrots, peeled and shredded
- 1 big raw beet, peeled and shredded, or 2 medium
- 1/4 red onion, cut thin
- 1/4 cup dried cranberries
- 1/2 cup goat cheese, crumbled
- 1/2 cup walnuts
- 1/2 cup Dijon Vinaigrette see recipe

INSTRUCTIONS
1. Toast walnuts.
2. In a large salad bowl, combine all ingredients.
3. Serve.

NUTRITION
- Calories: 275kcal
- Carbohydrates: 27g
- Protein: 10g
- Fat: 16g
- Saturated Fat: 5g
- Polyunsaturated Fat: 7g
- Monounsaturated Fat: 3g
- Cholesterol: 13mg
- Sodium: 446mg
- Potassium: 505mg
- Fiber: 5g
- Sugar: 20g
- Vitamin A: 5775IU
- Vitamin C: 8mg
- Calcium: 90mg
- Iron: 2mg

8.) Muhammara (Roasted Red Pepper and Walnut Dip):
Procedures can be found in page

9.) Garlic Soup with Egg and Croutons (Spain)

Spanish Garlic soup originated from the Castilian region in the heartland of Spain, notably in the tiny area of Zamora.

This soup has a simple basis and is thus amenable to various adaptations; it is typical to see different components in the soup besides the ones described in this recipe.

In ancient times, this Castilian soup was a customary lunch for modest people. It was an exceedingly inexpensive and highly soothing formula to transfer warmth throughout the body in chilly rural locations. It was consumed in the middle of the morning to preserve strength for the day, usually with one or two eggs broken within, which were cooked from the heat of the soup. Like other old recipes, it offered the extra function of using leftover bread from the day before.

In certain locations in Spain, this soup is one of the classic foods of Lent, because it doesn't require meat and its simplicity complements the religious focus. It is one significant aspect of the ceremonies included in the processions of Holy Week.

Like many popular meals, it's praised greatly; there are even poems devoted to the Spanish Garlic Soup. Here's one by Ventura de la Vega (1807-1865):

(Non-official translation)

Wide and deep bowl, made
Of clay (like myself) I threw it on the fire;
I fill it with water: a broken bread
In little chunks I will toss it in later;
With salt and powdered paprika,
Of pure virgin oil I water it;
Spanish garlic two chunks I peel
I bury them in the spongy dough.

A few elements of technique when you cook garlic soup.
- If you don't have stale bread, you may use toasted bread.

On a final point on technique, make sure you add the egg as soon as you turn off the heat so the egg will cook thoroughly in the soup.

PREP TIME	COOK TIME	TOTAL TIME	SERVINGS	CALORIES
5 Minutes	35 Minutes	40 Minutes	2	473 kcal

INGREDIENTS
- 2 slices stale bread (you may bake the bread if not stale), sliced into bite-sized pieces
- 2 eggs
- 6 cloves garlic
- 1 tsp sweet paprika
- 1-liter chicken broth or veggie broth homemade is ideal or shop purchased (low sodium)
- 1/4 cup extra virgin olive oil
- Salt and pepper, to taste (at least ½ teaspoon pepper)

INSTRUCTIONS
1. Peel the garlic and cut it into wedges.
2. Pour olive oil into a saucepan (enough to slightly cover the bottom) and heat over medium-high heat.
3. Add in the garlic and sauté until it begins to brown about 2-3 minutes.
4. Add the bread to the saucepan so that they are sautéed with the garlic and become saturated in the oil.
5. Turn the heat to low and add the paprika. Pour in the broth and whisk.

6. Bring the soup to a low boil and then cook on a low simmer for about 25 minutes. It is done when the bread is soft and the soup has a deep brown hue.
7. Salt and pepper, to taste adding at least ½ teaspoon pepper.
8. Remove the soup from the stove and quickly crack the eggs within so that they are cooked with the remaining heat. Stir the eggs into the soup. Eat warm.

NUTRITION
- Calories: 473kcal
- Carbohydrates: 24g
- Protein: 19g
- Fat: 35g
- Saturated Fat: 6g
- Polyunsaturated Fat: 5g
- Monounsaturated Fat: 23g
- Trans Fat: 1g
- Polyunsaturated
- Cholesterol: 164mg
- Sodium: 361mg
- Potassium: 601mg
- Fiber: 2g
- Sugar: 3g
- Vitamin A: 732IU
- Vitamin C: 3mg
- Calcium: 102mg
- Iron: 3mg

10.)Avocado Salad with Cucumber and Radish
Tired of eating the same old salads? This Mediterranean Diet-inspired avocado salad will get you thrilled again! It has a fantastic crunch to it and is full of healthy fats from avocado and extra virgin olive oil. It's also a terrific weight loss dish as it

includes satisfying fats but still is low in calories due to the veggies. All in all, don't be shocked if this becomes your new favorite salad!

The Best Avocado Salad
The greatest avocado salads are ones that use fully ripened avocados and balance off the smoothness of the avocado and olive oil with a little crispness. I like to buy avocados at the shop when they are extremely green so I can choose to utilize them at the appropriate moment for dishes like this. Also, throwing in items like radishes will balance out the textures of the meal.

PREP TIME	TOTAL TIME	SERVINGS	CALORIES
15 Minutes	15 Minutes	4	188 kcal

INGREDIENTS
- 2 medium radishes, chopped 1 big cucumber, split into quarters lengthwise and then chopped 1/4 cup red onion, chopped 1 ripe avocado, sliced into tiny bits.
- 1/4 cup chopped fresh parsley
- 1/2 lemon juice
- 1/2 tsp dried dill
- 3 tbsp extra virgin olive oil salt, to taste

INSTRUCTIONS
1. Add all ingredients to a large salad bowl.
2. Toss thoroughly and serve.

NUTRITION
- Calories: 188kcal
- Carbohydrates: 7g
- Protein: 2g

- Fat: 18g
- Saturated Fat: 3g
- Polyunsaturated Fat: 2g
- Monounsaturated Fat: 13g
- Sodium: 9mg
- Potassium: 387mg
- Fiber: 4g
- Sugar: 2g
- Vitamin A: 448IU
- Vitamin C: 15mg
- Calcium: 26mg
- Iron: 1mg

Chapter 7

15 Mediterranean Diet Dinner Plan and Recipes for Lowering Cholesterol

1.)Winter Vegetable Mulligatawny Soup

Our vegetarian version of the Indian-inspired British colonial soup incorporates parsnip and squash to keep it substantial and delicious.

Active: 25 minutes
Total: 50 minutes
Servings: 4
Nutrition Profile: Dairy-Free Egg-Free Heart Healthy High Fiber Low-Calorie Nut-Free Soy-Free Vegan

INGREDIENT

- 3 tablespoons extra-virgin olive oil, split
- 1 medium onion, finely chopped
- 2 medium carrots, finely chopped
- 1 medium parsnip, peeled and coarsely chopped
- 4 cups peeled diced acorn squash or butternut squash
- 1 medium green apple, peeled and coarsely chopped
- 1 tablespoon curry powder
- 3 cloves garlic, minced, divided
- 1 teaspoon grated fresh ginger
- 4 cups low-sodium vegetable broth
- 1 (14-ounce) can of no-salt-added diced tomatoes
- ½ cup red lentils picked over and rinsed
- 2 whole-wheat naan flatbreads, half ¼ cup chopped fresh cilantro, plus extra for garnish

INSTRUCTIONS

1. Preheat the oven to 375°F. Line a baking pan with foil.

2. Heat 2 tablespoons of oil in a large skillet over medium heat until it shimmers. Add onion, carrots, and parsnip and simmer until the onions are transparent for about 6 minutes. Add squash, apple, curry powder, 2 cloves garlic, and ginger and simmer, stirring, until aromatic, 1 to 2 minutes. Add broth, tomatoes, and lentils and stir to mix. Bring to a boil. Reduce heat to maintain a moderate simmer, cover, and cook until the squash and lentils are cooked for about 20 minutes.

3. Meanwhile, brush one side of each naan with the remaining 1 tablespoon of oil. Sprinkle with the remaining 1 clove of garlic and place on the prepared baking sheet. Bake until warmed, 5 to 6 minutes. Remove from the oven and sprinkle with cilantro.

4. Gently mash part of the soup with a potato masher to get the desired consistency. (Alternatively, put half the soup in a blender and purée. Use caution when combining heated liquids.) Garnish the soup with cilantro and serve with the naan..

Nutrition Facts

Serving Size: around 2 cups soup & 1/2 naan Per Serving: 487 calories; fat 15g; cholesterol 1mg; sodium 406mg; carbs 76g; dietary fiber 14g; protein 14g; sugars 17g; niacin equivalents 4mg; saturated fat 3g; vitamin a iu 7440IU; vitamin b6 1mg; potassium 983mg.

2.)Seared Tuna with Bulgur & Chickpea Salad

This nutritious tuna dish mixes fresh fish, olive oil, lemon juice, fresh herbs, and chickpeas. Cooking for two? Flake the two leftover tuna steaks and mix them with the remaining bulgur salad, then serve over lettuce for lunch the next day.

Active: 15 minutes

Total: 45 minutes
Servings: 4
Nutrition Profile: Dairy-Free Diabetes Appropriate Egg Free

INGREDIENTS

- ½ cup bulgur
- ¼ cup extra-virgin olive oil, split
- 4 tablespoons grated lemon zest, divided
- ½ cup lemon juice, split
- ½ teaspoon salt, divided
- ¼ teaspoon ground pepper
- 1 (15-ounce) can of no-salt-added chickpeas
- ¼ cup chopped fresh Italian parsley
- ¼ cup chopped fresh mint
- 1 pound tuna, sliced into 4 steaks (see Tip)
- 1 medium yellow onion, thinly sliced
- ¼ cup chopped fresh dill

INSTRUCTIONS

1. Bring a pot of water to a boil. Place bulgur in a large heatproof bowl. Add boiling water to cover by 2 inches. Let stand for 30 minutes. Drain any surplus water.

2. Mix the bulgur with 2 Tbsp. oil, 2 tsp. lemon zest, 1/4 cup lemon juice, 1/4 tsp. salt, and pepper. Add chickpeas, parsley, and mint; mix to blend. Set aside.

3. Heat the remaining 2 Tbsp. oil in a large skillet over medium-high heat. Add tuna steaks and sauté until gently browned on one side, 2 to 3 minutes. Flip the tuna and heat until gently browned on the other side. Transfer to a plate.

4. Reduce heat to medium. Add onion to the pan and simmer, turning periodically, until transparent, about 5 minutes. Reduce heat to medium-low. Return the tuna steaks to the pan, cover, and cook, flipping once until the tuna begins to

flake when examined with a fork (it will be slightly pink in the middle), 3 to 4 minutes on each side.

5.   Meanwhile, mix dill with the remaining 1/4 cup lemon juice and 1/4 tsp. salt in a small dish.

6.   Transfer the tuna to a serving plate. Spoon the onions over the tuna and drizzle with the lemon juice-dill combination. Sprinkle with the remaining 2 tsp. lemon zest and serve with the bulgur salad.

Tip: Ask at the seafood counter whether your fishmonger can cut 1 lb. of tuna into four 4-oz. steaks.

To make ahead: Prepare bulgur (Step 1) and refrigerate for up to 2 days.

Nutrition Facts
Serving Size: 1 tuna steak + 3/4 cup bulgur salad
Per Serving: 459 calories; protein 35.9g; carbs 43.2g; dietary fiber 8.2g; sugars 2.1g; fat 16.2g; saturated fat 2.4g; cholesterol 44.2mg; vitamin a iu 689.9IU; vitamin c 26.7mg; folate 102.3mcg; calcium 73.9mg; iron 3.8mg; magnesium 109.9mg; potassium 880.5mg; sodium 556.6mg.

3.)Peppery Barbecue-Glazed Shrimp with Vegetables & Orzo

In this healthy BBQ shrimp dish, shrimp are seasoned with a peppery spice combination and served with zucchini, peppers, and whole-grain orzo for a tasty and quick supper that's done in just 30 minutes. The shrimp and carrots are cooked in the same skillet, so cleaning is a cinch too.

Recipe summary:
Active: 30 minutes
Total: 30 minutes

INGREDIENTS

- 1 pound peeled and deveined jumbo shrimp, thawed if frozen (see Tip)
- 1 teaspoon paprika
- ½ teaspoon garlic powder
- ½ teaspoon dried oregano, crushed
- ¼ teaspoon ground pepper
- ⅛ teaspoon cayenne pepper
- 1 cup whole-grain orzo
- 3 scallions
- 2 tablespoons olive oil, divided
- 2 cups finely chopped zucchini
- 1 cup roughly chopped bell pepper
- ½ cup finely sliced celery
- 1 cup cherry tomatoes, halved
- ½ teaspoon salt
- 2 teaspoons barbecue sauce
- Lemon wedges for serving

INSTRUCTIONS

1. Place shrimp in a medium bowl. Combine paprika, garlic powder, oregano, pepper, and cayenne in a small bowl. Sprinkle the spice mixture over the shrimp; toss to coat and put aside.

2. Bring a large pot of water to a boil. Cook orzo according to package directions; drain. Return to the heated pot; cover and keep warm.

3. Meanwhile, slice onions, separating white and green sections. Heat 1 tablespoon of oil in a medium pan over medium-high heat. Add the scallion whites, zucchini, bell pepper, and celery; cook, turning occasionally until the veggies are crisp-tender, about 5 minutes. Add tomatoes;

heat until softened, 2 to 3 minutes longer. Add the veggies to the saucepan with the orzo. Add salt; toss to mix.

4. In the same skillet, heat the remaining 1 tablespoon of oil over medium heat. Add the shrimp; cook, flipping once, until opaque, 4 to 6 minutes. Drizzle with barbeque sauce. Cook and stir until the shrimp are coated for approximately 1 minute.

5. Serve the shrimp with the veggie combination. Top with scallion leaves and serve with lemon wedges, if preferred.

Tip: Frozen shrimp thawed rapidly. Place frozen shrimp in a large basin with cold water. Let stand for 20 minutes.

Nutrition Facts

Serving Size: 2 cups Per Serving: 360 calories; protein 30.1g; carbohydrates 40.6g; dietary fiber 9.5g; sugars 7.2g; fat 8.9g; saturated fat 1.2g; cholesterol 182.6mg; vitamin a iu 2098IU; vitamin c 66.4mg; folate 50.4mcg; calcium 109.3mg; iron 1.5mg; magnesium 66.2mg; potassium 734.1mg; sodium 553.8mg; thiamin 0.1mg; added sugar 3g.
Exchanges: 3 lean proteins, 2 starch, 1 fat, 1 vegetable.

4.) Vegetable Weight-Loss Soup

A huge bowl of delicious vegetable soup can leave you content for hours without ingesting a lot of calories, which is excellent when attempting to lose weight. Plus, it's an easy way to raise your veggie portions for the day—something all of us might benefit from. Top with a dollop of pesto before enjoying this delightful vegetable soup and consider serving with a loaf of toasted whole-wheat bread to further finish out the meal.

Recipe Summary
Active: 45 minutes

Total: 1 hour
Servings: 8

How to Make the Best Vegetable Soup
All veggies are great additions to the vegetable soup because vegetables give health advantages. Nearly all veggies include fiber which helps keep you full and happy and can aid in weight reduction. In our vegetable soup, we add onions, carrots, celery, green beans, kale, zucchini, tomatoes, and garlic, but there's an opportunity to get creative! Here are some additional veggies that work well:

Leeks, fennel, potatoes, sweet potatoes, sweet peppers, mushrooms, eggplant, peas, corn, spinach, Swiss chard

A decent rule of thumb if you feel adventurous is to choose a few veggies from the allium family (think onions, leeks, and garlic) to start to create the taste. Move next to veggies that provide bulk like carrots, peas, and squash, and lastly, one or two soft leafy greens that add texture like spinach or kale. You may also mix up the broth you use. Use vegetable, no-chicken, or mushroom broth for a vegetarian soup, or chicken or beef broth for a meatier flavor.

Can I Make Vegetable Soup In The Slow Cooker?
We prepare this vegetable soup on the stovetop, but a slow cooker comes in useful for hectic days. Luckily, you can make this vegetable soup dish in the slow cooker! For those hectic days when you need to plan, try out the slow-cooker version of this healthful soup.

How to Store Vegetable Soup
It's simple to have a fast and nutritious lunch or dinner if you've got vegetable soup on hand. Shortly prepare through Step 3 and chill for

up to 5 days or divide the soup and freeze for up to 6 months; finish Step 4 just before serving.

INGREDIENTS
- 2 tablespoons extra-virgin olive oil
- 1 medium onion, chopped
- 2 medium carrots, chopped
- 2 stalks of celery, chopped
- 12 ounces fresh green beans, sliced into 1/2-inch pieces
- 2 cloves garlic, minced
- 8 cups of no-salt-added chicken broth or low-sodium vegetable broth
- 2 (15-ounce) cans of low-sodium cannellini or other white beans, washed
- 4 cups chopped kale
- 2 medium zucchini, chopped
- 4 Roma tomatoes, seeded and chopped
- 2 tablespoons red wine vinegar
- ¾ teaspoon salt
- ½ teaspoon ground pepper
- 8 teaspoons premade pesto

INSTRUCTIONS
1. Heat oil in a big saucepan over medium-high heat. Add onion, carrot, celery, green beans, and garlic. Cook, stirring regularly until the veggies begin to soften, approximately 10 minutes.
2. Add broth and bring to a boil. Reduce heat to a simmer and cook, stirring periodically, until the veggies are tender, about 10 minutes more.
3. Add white beans, kale, zucchini, tomatoes, vinegar, salt, and pepper. Increase heat to bring to a simmer; cook until the zucchini and kale have softened, about 10 minutes.
4. Top each dish of soup with 1 teaspoon of pesto.

Nutrition Facts

Serving Size: 1 3/4 cups each Per Serving: 225 calories; protein 12.7g; carbohydrates 27.8g; dietary fiber 7.6g; sugars 5.3g; fat 8.4g; saturated fat 1.4g; vitamin a iu 4134.1IU; vitamin c 30.3mg; folate 52.3mcg; calcium 106.4mg; iron 3.1mg; magnesium 88.6mg; potassium 865.8mg; sodium 406mg; thiamin 0.7mg.

Exchanges: 2 vegetables, 1 fat, 1 lean-fat protein, 1 starch

5.)White Bean Soup with Pasta

We use mirepoix—a blend of onion, celery, and carrots—to flavor this white bean soup. Keep a store-bought bag of the mixture in your freezer to guarantee you always have some on hand without worrying about it going bad.

Recipe Summary
Active: 15 minutes
Total: 25 minutes
Servings: 6

How to Make White Bean Soup with Pasta
This hearty soup is the perfect winter supper! Here are tips on how to create it:

- Use Frozen Mirepoix

Mirepoix is a blend of chopped onion, celery, and carrots. It's often used as a flavored basis for stocks, soups, and stews. For this dish, we use frozen mirepoix which is easy to have on hand and cuts down on prep time. You may prepare your mirepoix by slicing the onion, celery, and carrots in a 2:1:1 ratio—two parts onion, one part celery, and one part carrot. Reserve 1 ½ cups of it for this recipe and freeze the remainder.

- Choose the White Beans

We use cannellini beans for this recipe, but you can use any type of white beans such as navy beans or great northern beans. Just make sure to use low-sodium canned white beans.

- Cook the Pasta Separately

Cooking the pasta separately prevents it from overcooking and becoming soggy. If you're making this soup in advance, storing the soup and pasta separately keeps the pasta al dente before reheating. You can refrigerate the soup and pasta in separate airtight containers for up to 3 days.

INGREDIENTS
- 1 tablespoon extra-virgin olive oil
- 1 ½ cups frozen mirepoix (diced onion, celery, and carrots).
- 2 cloves garlic, minced
- 1 teaspoon Italian seasoning
- 1 teaspoon salt
- ¼ teaspoon crushed red pepper
- ¼ teaspoon ground pepper
- 1 (28-ounce) can of no-salt-added diced tomatoes
- 2 cups low-sodium no-chicken broth or chicken broth
- 1 (15-ounce) can of low-sodium cannellini beans, washed

- 8 ounces little whole-wheat pasta, such as elbows
- 1 ½ cups frozen cut-leaf spinach
- 4 tablespoons grated Parmesan cheese

INSTRUCTIONS
1. Put a big pot of water on to boil.
2. Heat oil in a big saucepan over medium-high heat. Add mirepoix and simmer, stirring, until softened, approximately 3 minutes. Add garlic, Italian seasoning, salt, crushed red pepper, and ground pepper and simmer, stirring, until fragrant, approximately 1 minute. Add tomatoes and their juices, broth, and beans, and bring to a

boil. Reduce heat to maintain a brisk simmer. Cover and boil, stirring periodically until the tomatoes begin to break down, approximately 10 minutes.

3. Meanwhile, cook pasta in boiling water for 1 minute shorter than the package guidelines. Drain.
4. Stir spinach into the soup. Stir in the spaghetti immediately before serving. Serve topped with Parmesan.

EQUIPMENTS
- Large saucepan
- large pot

To make ahead: Refrigerate soup and pasta separately for up to 3 days.

Nutrition Facts
Serving Size: 1 1/3 cups Per Serving: 277 calories; fat 5g; cholesterol 3mg; sodium 576mg; carbs 49g; dietary fiber 9g; protein 12g; sugars 7g; niacin equivalents 3mg; saturated fat 1g; vitamin a iu 2217IU; potassium 329mg.

6.) Spicy Shrimp, Vegetable & Couscous Bowls
We enjoy the chewy texture and huge size of pearl couscous (often termed Israeli couscous) as the basis of these bowls.

Recipe Summary
Active: 20 minutes
Total: 20 minutes
Servings: 4

INGREDIENTS
- 1 ½ cups whole-wheat pearl couscous
- 1 small red bell pepper, chopped
- ½ cup snow peas, trimmed and sliced
- 3 tablespoons sliced fresh basil, divided

- 3 tablespoons sliced fresh mint, divided
- 1 cup chopped fresh cilantro
- 2 tablespoons lime juice
- 1 tablespoon rice vinegar
- 1 tablespoon water
- 1 ½ tablespoon sambal oelek
- 1 ½ teaspoon grated fresh ginger
- 1 large clove of garlic, crushed and peeled
- ½ teaspoon ground pepper, divided
- ⅛ teaspoon salt
- 5 tablespoons grapeseed oil, split
- 1 pound big raw shrimp (16-20 count), peeled and deveined

INSTRUCTIONS

1. Cook couscous according to package guidelines. Drain, rinse and place in a big dish. Add bell pepper, snow peas, and 2 teaspoons each of basil and mint.

2. Meanwhile, mix cilantro, lime juice, vinegar, water, sambal oelek, ginger, garlic, 1/4 teaspoon pepper, and salt in a blender. Blend until smooth. With the motor running, softly sprinkle in 4 tablespoons of oil. Set aside 2 tablespoons of the dressing. Toss the remaining dressing with the couscous and veggies to coat.

3. Heat the remaining 1 tablespoon oil in a large pan over high heat. Pat shrimp dry and sprinkle with the remaining 1/4 teaspoon pepper. Add to the pan and cook, flipping once, until barely cooked through, about 2 minutes per side. Serve the shrimp and couscous combination with the leftover 2 tablespoons of dressing and the remaining 1 tablespoon of each basil and mint.

Tip: Sambal oelek is a thick Indonesian sauce made with chilies, vinegar, and salt that provides a fiery bite to the dressing here. Find it in well-stocked grocery stores or specialist Asian grocery stores.

Use the rest of that jar in stir-fries, noodle meals, or in place of your favorite spicy sauce.

Nutrition Facts

Serving Size: 3 oz. shrimp & 1 cup couscous salad

Per Serving: 478 calories; fat 18g; cholesterol 159mg; sodium 236mg; carbohydrates 52g; dietary fiber 6g; protein 28g; sugars 1g; saturated fat 2g; vitamin a iu 1145 IU; potassium 365mg.

7.)Chickpea Pasta with Mushrooms & Kale

Loading up your spaghetti with veggies like the kale and mushrooms above is not only tasty but also makes the meal more gratifying.

Recipe Summary

Active: 30 minutes

Total: 30 minutes

Servings: 4

INGREDIENTS

- 8 ounces chickpea rotini or penne (see Tip) (see Tip)
- ¼ cup extra-virgin olive oil
- 2 big cloves garlic, sliced
- Pinch of crushed red pepper
- 8 cups chopped kale
- 8 ounces cremini mushrooms, quartered
- ½ teaspoon dried thyme
- ½ teaspoon salt

INSTRUCTIONS

1. Cook pasta according to package guidelines. Reserve 1 cup of the cooking water, then drain.
2. Meanwhile, heat oil in a large pan over medium heat. Add garlic and crushed red pepper; simmer, stirring once, until

fragrant, approximately 1 minute. Add kale, mushrooms, thyme, and salt; simmer, stirring occasionally, until the veggies are tender, approximately 5 minutes.

3. Stir in the pasta and enough of the reserved water to coat; simmer, stirring, until mixed and heated, approximately 1 minute more. Serve topped with Parmesan, if preferred.

Tip: We picked chickpea pasta for this recipe instead of whole-wheat because it's filled with plenty of fiber, protein, and nutrients—some brands contain more than 40% of your daily necessary fiber, plus 20 grams of protein per serving. Look for it among other gluten-free kinds of pasta.

Nutrition Facts
Serving Size: 1 1/2 cups Per Serving: 340 calories; protein 17g; carbs 38g; dietary fiber 10g; sugars 7g; fat 18g; saturated fat 2g; sodium 366mg; potassium 717mg.

8.) Butternut Squash & Black Bean Enchiladas
A crunchy, lemony slaw contrasts wonderfully with the enchiladas' creamy squash filling.

Recipe Summary
Active: 25 minutes
 Total: 45 mins
Servings: 4

INGREDIENTS
- 3 tablespoons extra-virgin olive oil, split
- 3 cups chopped peeled butternut squash
- 2 medium poblano peppers, seeded and chopped
- 1 medium onion, chopped
- 1 (14-ounce) can of no-salt-added black beans, rinsed

- 4 tablespoons chopped fresh cilantro, divided, plus extra for serving
- 1 tablespoon ancho chile powder
- 8 corn tortillas, warmed
- 1 (10-ounce) can of enchilada sauce (see Tip)
- ½ cup shredded Monterey Jack cheese
- 2 cups shredded cabbage
- 1 tablespoon lime juice

INSTRUCTIONS

1. Preheat the oven to 425°F. Lightly cover a 7-by-11-inch baking dish with cooking spray.
2. Heat 2 tablespoons of oil in a large pan over medium heat. Add squash and cook, covered, stirring occasionally, until soft and lightly browned, 8 to 10 minutes. Add peppers and onion and cook, uncovered, stirring occasionally, until soft, approximately 5 minutes. Remove from heat and toss in beans, 2 tablespoons of cilantro, and chili powder. Let cool for 5 minutes
3. Place about 1/2 cup of the squash mixture in each tortilla and roll. Place, seam-side down, in the prepared baking dish. Top with enchilada sauce. Sprinkle it with cheese and cover with foil. Bake until bubbling, approximately 15 minutes. Remove foil and bake for another 5 minutes.
4. Meanwhile, combine cabbage with lime juice, the remaining 1 tablespoon of oil, and 2 tablespoons of cilantro. Serve the enchiladas topped with the slaw and extra cilantro, if preferred.

Tip: Store-bought enchilada sauce is a fast and simple way to add a ton of flavor to a dish, but it may be heavy in sodium, so search for one that has fewer than 300 milligrams per serving.

Nutrition Facts
Serving Size: 2 enchiladas & 1/2 cup slaw
Per Serving: 428 calories; protein 13g; carbs 58g; dietary fiber 11g; sugars 6g; fat 17g; saturated fat 4g; cholesterol 13mg; sodium 491mg; potassium 779mg.

9.) Red Lentil Soup with Saffron

This hearty red lentil soup combines spices prevalent in Persian cuisine: turmeric, cumin, and saffron. Enjoy it with a warm baguette or steaming rice.

Recipe Summary
 Active: 20 minutes
Total: 40 minutes
Servings: 8

INGREDIENTS

- 3 tablespoons extra-virgin olive oil
- 2 medium carrots, finely diced
- 2 stalks of celery, finely diced
- 1 big onion, coarsely diced
- 3 cloves garlic, minced
- 1 tablespoon tomato paste
- ½ teaspoon ground cumin
- ¼ teaspoon crushed saffron threads
- ¼ teaspoon ground turmeric
- 4 cups low-sodium no-chicken or chicken broth
- 1 ½ cups water, plus more as needed
- 1 pound red lentils (2 cups), picked over and washed
- 5 ounces spinach, finely chopped
- 1 teaspoon kosher salt
- 1 teaspoon ground pepper

INSTRUCTIONS

1. Heat oil in a big heavy saucepan over medium heat. Add carrots, celery, and onion and heat until starting to soften, 7 to 10 minutes. (Do not brown.) Stir in garlic, tomato paste, cumin, saffron, and turmeric, and simmer for 1 minute.

2. Add broth, water, lentils, spinach, salt, and pepper. Bring to a simmer. Adjust heat to maintain a simmer, cover, and cook, tossing as required to prevent sticking, until the lentils and veggies are cooked, 15 to 20 minutes. Add extra water if desired.

3. Garnish with yogurt and mint if preferred.

To make ahead: Refrigerate for up to 3 days or freeze for up to 3 months.

Nutrition Facts

Serving Size: generous 1 cup Per Serving: 280 calories; protein 15g; carbs 42g; dietary fiber 8g; sugars 2g; fat 7g; saturated fat 1g; sodium 364mg; potassium 512mg.

10.) Vegan Mushroom Bolognese

This Bolognese sauce recipe is based on Marcella Hazan's Essentials of Classic Italian Cooking. We change up the beef and pork with button mushrooms to keep this traditional comfort dish vegan yet hefty with umami flavor. And although other recipes call for red wine, this dish stays with Hazan's white wine pick.

Recipe Summary
Active: 15 minutes
Total: 1 hour
Servings: 4

INGREDIENTS

- 1 pound white button mushrooms, split
- 2 teaspoons light vegetable oil
- ½ cup chopped onion
- ⅔ cup sliced carrots
- ⅔ cup chopped celery
- Pinch of salt
- ½ cup unsweetened oat milk
- ¼ teaspoon nutmeg
- ½ cup dry white wine
- 1 cup canned crushed tomatoes
- 1 pound whole-wheat pasta, ideally ancient-grain (see Tips)
- butter, cut into 5 pieces

Vegan Parmesan cheese for garnish (see Tips)

INSTRUCTIONS

1. Put half the mushrooms in a food processor and pulse until coarsely chopped. Chop the remaining mushrooms into 1/4-inch pieces.

2. Heat oil in a big heavy saucepan over medium heat. Add onion; cook, stirring regularly, until transparent. Add carrots and celery; simmer, stirring, until softened, 3 to 4 minutes. Add the minced and chopped mushrooms and salt; simmer, stirring until the mushrooms start to release their juices. Add oat milk; simmer, stirring, until it evaporates. Stir in nutmeg. Add wine; simmer, stirring, until it evaporates. Add tomatoes and bring to a boil.

3. Lower the heat to maintain a gentle simmer; cook for 45 minutes, stirring periodically. (If the sauce seems dry, add boiling water, 1/4 cup at a time.)

4. Meanwhile, bring a big pot of water to a boil. Cook pasta according to package directions; drain. Serve the pasta

topped with the sauce and garnished with Parmesan, if preferred.

Tips: Look for fiber-rich ancient-grain pasta, such as Gustiamo's Sicilian Tumminia Busiate.

Nutrition Facts
Serving Size: 1 1/2 cups Per Serving: 393 calories; protein 14.4g; carbs 63g; dietary fiber 9.6g; sugars 8.2g; fat 10.2g; saturated fat 1.5g; vitamin a iu 3777IU; vitamin c 11.2mg; folate 73.8mcg; calcium 63.8mg; iron 4.2mg; magnesium 113.8mg; potassium 830.5mg; sodium 190.8mg.

11.) Lemon-Herb Salmon with Caponata & Farro

Dig into your farmers' market harvest to create this colorful and healthful Mediterranean diet supper meal that's filled with veggies. Feel free to switch in any vegetables or cook up another healthy grain, such as brown rice. Serve with a glass of your favorite red wine.

Recipe Summary
Total: 50 minutes
Servings: 4

INGREDIENTS
- 2 cups water
- ⅔ cup farro
- 1 medium eggplant, cut into 1-inch cubes
- 1 red bell pepper, sliced into 1-inch pieces
- 1 summer squash, sliced into 1-inch chunks
- 1 small onion, sliced into 1-inch chunks
- 1 ½ cups cherry tomatoes
- 3 tablespoons extra-virgin olive oil

- ¾ teaspoon salt, divided
- ½ teaspoon ground pepper, divided
- 2 tablespoons capers, washed and chopped
- 1 tablespoon red wine vinegar
- 2 teaspoons honey
- 1 ¼ pound wild salmon (see Tips) split into 4 parts
- 1 teaspoon lemon zest
- ½ teaspoon Italian seasoning
- Lemon wedges for serving

INSTRUCTIONS

1. Position racks in the upper and lower thirds of the oven; preheat to 450 degrees F. Line 2 rimmed baking pans with foil and cover with cooking spray.
2. Bring water and farro to a boil in a saucepan. Reduce heat to medium, cover, and simmer until barely tender, approximately 30 minutes. Drain if required.
3. Meanwhile, toss eggplant, bell pepper, squash, onion, and tomatoes with oil, 1/2 teaspoon salt, and 1/4 teaspoon pepper in a large bowl. Divide amongst the prepared baking sheets. Roast on the top and lower racks, tossing once midway until the veggies are soft and beginning to brown, about 25 minutes. Return them to the basin. Stir in capers, vinegar, and honey.
4. Season salmon with lemon zest, Italian seasoning, and the remaining 1/4 teaspoon of each salt and pepper and place on one of the baking sheets. Roast on the bottom rack until barely cooked through, 6 to 12 minutes, depending on thickness. Serve the salmon with the farro, vegetable caponata, and lemon wedges.

Tips: Most wild salmon—and increasingly some farmed—is considered a sustainable choice. Get more info on sustainable seafood at seafoodwatch.org.

Nutrition Facts

Serving Size: 1 cup veggies, 1/2 cup farro, 4 oz. salmon
Per Serving: 450 calories; protein 34.8g; carbohydrates 41.2g;
dietary fiber 8.2g; sugars 12.5g; fat 17.3g; saturated fat 2.9g;
cholesterol 66.3mg; vitamin a iu 1737.5IU; vitamin c 54.6mg; folate
77.1mcg; calcium 112mg; iron 2.4mg; magnesium 82.7mg;
potassium 1109.1mg; sodium 562.1mg; added sugar 3g.
Exchanges: 1 1/2 starch, 3 veg, 2 fat, 4 lean protein.

12.) Beer-Battered Fish Tacos with Tomato & Avocado Salsa

Lovers of fried fish receive the taste without all the calories, and the
salsa provides a fresh, clean accent. To complete the Baja motif,
serve with black beans, some sliced mango, and a dollop of light
sour cream.

Recipe Summary
Total: 40 minutes
Servings: 2

INGREDIENTS

- 1 big tomato, chopped
- ¼ cup chopped red onion
- ½ jalapeno, minced
- 2-3 teaspoons lime juice
- ¼ teaspoon kosher salt
- ⅛ teaspoon freshly ground pepper
- ½ avocado, diced
- ¼ cup chopped fresh cilantro
- Pinch of cayenne, if desired
- Fish Tacos
- 3 tablespoons all-purpose flour
- ⅛ teaspoon ground cumin

- ⅛ teaspoon salt
- ⅛ teaspoon cayenne pepper, or to taste
- ⅓ cup beer
- 8 ounces tilapia fillet, cut crosswise into 1-inch wide strips
- 2 tablespoons canola oil
- 4 corn tortillas, warmed (see Tip)

INSTRUCTIONS

1. To prepare salsa: Combine tomato, onion, jalapeño, lime juice to taste, and kosher salt and pepper in a medium bowl. Stir in avocado and cilantro. Add cayenne (if using).
2. To prepare tacos: Combine flour, cumin, salt, and cayenne in a medium basin. Whisk in beer to produce a batter.
3. Coat tilapia chunks in the batter. Heat oil in a large nonstick skillet over medium-high heat. Letting excess batter drop back into the bowl, add the fish to the pan; cook until crispy and golden, 2 to 4 minutes on each side. Serve the fish with tortillas and salsa.

Tip: To reheat tortillas, wrap in just moist paper towels and microwave on High for 30 to 45 seconds or cover in foil and bake at 300 degrees F until steaming, 5 to 10 minutes.

To make ahead: Cover and refrigerate the salsa (Step 1) for up to 3 days.

Nutrition Facts
Serving Size: 2 tacos & around 3/4 cup salsa
Per Serving: 401 calories; protein 28.5g; carbs 39g; dietary fiber 8.3g; sugars 4.4g; fat 15.7g; saturated fat 2.3g; cholesterol 56.7mg; vitamin a iu 1042.3IU; vitamin c 28.3mg; folate 113.4mcg; calcium 77.2mg; iron 2.2mg; magnesium 97.3mg; potassium 974.3mg; sodium 406.5mg; thiamin 0.2mg.
Exchanges: 1 fruit, 1/2 other carbohydrate, 3 lean meat, 2 fat

13.) Baked Halibut with Brussels Sprouts & Quinoa Fish plus two sides? It appears luxurious but this nutritious supper comes ready in about 30 minutes.

Recipe Summary
Active: 15 minutes
Total: 30 minutes
Servings: 4

INGREDIENTS
- 1 pound Brussels sprouts, trimmed and sliced
- 1 fennel bulb, trimmed and sliced into strips
- 1 tablespoon plus 1 teaspoon olive oil, divided
- ½ teaspoon salt, divided
- ½ teaspoon ground pepper, divided
- 1 (1 pound) halibut fillet, split into 4 parts
- 4 cloves garlic, minced, divided
- 3 tablespoons lemon juice
- 2 tablespoons unsalted butter, melted
- 2 cups cooked quinoa
- ¼ cup chopped sun-dried tomatoes
- ¼ cup chopped pitted Kalamata olives
- 2 tablespoons chopped fresh Italian parsley or fennel fronds

INSTRUCTIONS
1. Position racks in the upper and bottom thirds of the oven; warm to 400 degrees F.
2. Combine Brussels sprouts, fennel, and 1 Tbsp. oil, and 1/4 tsp. each salt and pepper in a large bowl; toss to coat. Spread in a single layer on a large-rimmed baking sheet. Bake, stirring occasionally, until tender, 20 to 25 minutes.
3. Meanwhile, place halibut on another large-rimmed baking sheet and top with half of the garlic and the remaining 1/4

tsp. each salt and pepper. Combine lemon juice and melted butter in a small bowl. Drizzle or brush half of the mixture over the fish. Bake until the salmon is opaque and flakes readily with a fork, 12 to 15 minutes.

4. Meanwhile, mix quinoa, the remaining 1 tsp. oil, sun-dried tomatoes, olives, and parsley (or fennel fronds) in a medium bowl.

5. Add the remaining garlic to the lemon-butter combination. Pour the mixture over the veggies and bake for 1 minute more. Serve the halibut and veggies with the quinoa mixture.

Nutrition Facts
Serving Size: 3 oz. fish + 1 cup veggies + 1/2 cup quinoa
Per Serving: 406 calories; protein 29.7g; carbs 36.1g; dietary fiber 7.9g; sugars 5.1g; fat 17.1g; saturated fat 5.3g; cholesterol 70.8mg; vitamin a iu 1904.2IU; vitamin c 96.9mg; folate 145.9mcg; calcium 107.9mg; iron 3.8mg; magnesium 126.3mg; potassium 1378.7mg; sodium 560.1mg.

14.) Winter Kale & Quinoa Salad with Avocado
Precooked quinoa helps keep this nutritious salad dish quick and easy. Loaded with black beans, kale, and avocado, this recipe is as filling as it is nutritious. You can also make sweet potatoes and dress ahead.

Recipe Summary
Active: 15 mins
Total: 35 mins
Servings: 2

INGREDIENTS
- 1 small sweet potato, peeled and chopped into 1/2-inch pieces (1 1/2 cups)

- 2 ½ tablespoons olive oil, divided
- ½ avocado
- 1 tablespoon lime juice
- 1 clove garlic, peeled
- ½ teaspoon ground cumin
- ⅛ teaspoon salt
- ⅛ teaspoon ground pepper
- 1-2 tablespoons water
- 1 cup cooked quinoa (see Associated Recipes) (see Associated Recipes)
- ¾ cup no-salt-added canned black beans, rinsed
- 1 ½ cups chopped baby kale
- 2 tablespoons pepitas (see Tip)

1 scallion, chopped

INSTRUCTIONS
1. Preheat the oven to 400 degrees F.
2. Toss sweet potato and 1 tsp. oil on a large-rimmed baking sheet. Roast, tossing once halfway through, until soft, approximately 25 minutes.
3. Meanwhile, put the remaining 1 1/2 tsp. oil, avocado, lime juice, garlic, cumin, salt, pepper, and 1 Tbsp. water in a blender or food processor; process until smooth. Add 1 Tbsp. water, if required, to attain desired consistency.
4. Combine the sweet potato, quinoa, black beans, and kale in a medium bowl. Drizzle with the avocado dressing and gently toss to coat. Top with pepitas and scallion.

Tip: Pepitas (hulled pumpkin seeds) can be 8found in the bulk-foods section of natural-foods stores and Mexican groceries.

To make ahead: Prepare sweet potato (Steps 1-2) and dressing (Step 3). Refrigerate separately for up to 2 days.

Nutrition Facts

Serving Size: 1 1/4 cups salad + 3 Tbsp. dressing

Per Serving: 439 calories; protein 14.6g; carbs 54.4g; dietary fiber 13.8g; sugars 4.6g; fat 19.7g; saturated fat 2.8g; vitamin a iu 10580.9IU; vitamin c 25.3mg; folate 113.9mcg; calcium 121.5mg; iron 4.6mg; magnesium 191.2mg; potassium 993.6mg; sodium 252.6mg.

15.) Spicy Slaw Bowls with Shrimp & Edamame

The fast 10-minute Spicy Cabbage Slaw serves as the low-carb backbone in this veggie-packed lunch meal. Topped with high-protein edamame and shrimp, this hearty meal will help you power through the afternoon.

Recipe Summary

Active: 15 minutes

Total: 15 minutes

Servings: 4

INGREDIENTS

- Spicy Cabbage Slaw (see accompanying recipe) (see associated recipe)
- 2 cups frozen shelled edamame, thawed
- 1 medium avocado, diced
- ½ medium lime, juiced
- 12 ounces peeled cooked shrimp

INSTRUCTIONS

1. Prepare Spicy Cabbage Slaw. Add edamame; toss and set aside.

2. Toss avocado with lime juice in a small bowl.
3. Divide the slaw mixture among 4 containers. Top each with 1/4 of the shrimp (about 3 ounces) and 1/4 of the avocado. Cover and refrigerate until ready to eat.

To make ahead: Keep the cabbage mixture and dressing for the Spicy Cabbage Slaw separate and wait to combine until ready to eat. If using precooked frozen shrimp, wait to defrost the shrimp until you're ready to eat.

Nutrition Facts

Serving Size: 1 cup slaw, 1/2 cup edamame, 3 oz. shrimp & 1/4 avocado

Per Serving: 364 calories; protein 28.1g; carbohydrates 19.7g; dietary fiber 9.5g; sugars 3.4g; fat 18.8g; saturated fat 3.2g; cholesterol 136.9mg; vitamin a iu 525.5IU; vitamin c 11.6mg; folate 41mcg; calcium 111.8mg; iron 2.4mg; magnesium 44.6mg; potassium 472.5mg; sodium 302.8mg.

Exchanges: 3 1/2 lean-protein, 3 fat, 1 vegetable, 1/2 starch.

Chapter 8

Mediterranean Dessert Recipes

Any decent eating plan has to contain desserts, even when you're attempting to get healthier. Base your desserts on fruits, veggies, and nuts. These Mediterranean dessert dishes are a terrific way to get started.

Galatopita

This is a simple pudding that makes a nice weeknight treat.

Makes 10 servings

INGREDIENTS
- 4½ cups milk
- 1 cup semolina flour
- ½ cup honey
- 5 eggs
- Olive oil cooking spray Dash of vanilla

INSTRUCTIONS
1. Preheat the oven to 375 degrees F.
2. Whisk the eggs.
3. Place all the ingredients in a pan.
4. Cook the pudding over medium heat while regularly stirring until the custard is thick.
5. Grease a baking pan with cooking spray and pour in the custard.
6. Bake for about an hour.
7. Turn off the heat and allow the pudding to cool for another 15 minutes.

Nutrition Facts (Per Serving) Calories: 198 Fat: 4.6 g Sat Fat: 2.1 g Carbohydrates: 31.7 g Fiber: 0.7 g Sugar: 19 g Protein: 8.5 g Sodium: 83 mg

Pudding Parfait
Makes 4 servings

INGREDIENTS
- 1 package Jell-O sugar-free
- fat-free instant chocolate pudding
- 2 cups skim milk
- ½ cup sliced strawberries
- 1 banana, sliced
- ½ cup blueberries

INSTRUCTIONS
1. In a large bowl, stir the instant pudding mix together with cold milk.
2. Once it's blended, cover the pudding and refrigerate. It should be set within 30 minutes.
3. Set up four dessert glasses or dishes. On the bottom of each one, add a few berries. Cover with pudding, and then arrange a layer of bananas in the cups or bowls. Add more pudding, and place a layer of berries.
4. Do this until all the pudding and fruit are evenly distributed.

Nutrition Facts (Per Serving) Calories: 96 Fat: 0.2 g Sat Fat: 0 g Carbohydrates: 18.8 g Fiber: 1.8 g Sugar: 12.3 g Protein: 4.6 g Sodium: 143 mg.

Fruit and Yogurt Lasagna

This is a delicious dessert and if you have a little bit of fruit and yogurt behind, it also makes a great snack in the middle of the morning when you're not sure you'll make it to lunch.

Makes 4 serving

INGREDIENTS
- 4 dessert cups
- 1 cup blueberries
- 1 cup strawberries
- 1 cup blackberries
- 2 cups plain Greek yogurt
- ¼ cup crushed walnuts

INSTRUCTIONS
1. Place a spoonful of yogurt in each cup. Then, make layers of fruit and yogurt.
2. First, do the strawberries and then add yogurt. Then, try the blueberries followed by yogurt, and then the blackberries.
3. Top each dessert cup with yogurt and sprinkle with crumbled walnuts.

Nutrition Facts (Per Serving) Calories: 116 Fat: 3.2 g Sat Fat: 1.4 g Carbohydrates: 14.7 g Fiber: 3.7 g Sugar: 10.1 g Protein: 8.8 g Sodium: 26 mg.

Banana Balls
These make a fantastic dessert or snack. They're fast and easy to make, and you get a chocolate snack without overindulging. This isn't an everyday pleasure, but something you can enjoy while following the Mediterranean eating plan.

Makes 8 servings

INGREDIENTS

- 3 ripe bananas
- ½ cup peanut butter
- ¼ cup dark chocolate chips
- ¼ cup whole grain oats

INSTRUCTIONS

1. Preheat the oven to 350 degrees F.
2. Mash the bananas until they're smooth. Stir in the peanut butter, chocolate chips, and oats.
3. Roll into balls and set on a baking pan.
4. Bake for 20 minutes, until the outside starts to brown.

Nutrition Facts (Per Serving) Calories: 162 Fat: 9.5 g Sat Fat: 2.4 g Carbohydrates: 17.6 g Fiber: 2.4 g Sugar: 9 g Protein: 5.1 g Sodium: 75 mg.

Chocolate Hazelnut Baklava
Makes 20 servings

INGREDIENTS FOR THE PASTRY

- 2 cups hazelnuts
- 5 oz. semisweet chocolate, chopped
- 3 tbsp. honey
- ½ tsp. cinnamon
- ½ pound. phyllo dough
- ½ cup olive oil

INGREDIENTS FOR THE SYRUP

- 1 cup sugar
- ½ cup water
- ¼ cup honey
- 1 ¼ tsp. instant espresso coffee
- 2 tbsp. Kahlua liquor

INSTRUCTIONS

1. Preheat the oven to 350 degrees F.
2. Finely chop the hazelnuts, chocolate, cinnamon, and sugar in a food processor. Set aside.
3. Roll out the phyllo dough and cut it into 9" by 9" squares. Place a moist towel over the phyllo dough.
4. Grease a square 9" baking pan. Lay a phyllo square on the pan and brush with olive oil.
5. Keep adding 6 additional layers of phyllo squares, brushing each layer with the oil.
6. Transfer the ground hazelnut/chocolate combination over the phyllo.
7. Layer and oil the remaining phyllo squares.
8. Using a sharp knife, cut the phyllo into 9 squares. Halve each of the squares to produce triangles.
9. Bake for 35 minutes and let cool.

INSTRUCTIONS FOR THE SYRUP

1. To make the syrup, pour all ingredients, except the Kahlua, into a pan and bring to a boil. Reduce heat and let simmer until the syrup thickens.
2. Remove from heat and mix in the Kahlua. Pour the hot syrup over the baklava.
3. Let settle for 5–6 hours before serving.

Nutrition Facts (Per Serving) Calories: 218 Fat: 12.4 g Sat Fat: 2.5 g Carbohydrates: 27.8 g Fiber: 1.4 g Sugar: 20.3 g Protein: 2.3 g Sodium: 56 mg